Best of Luck

HAS

man@the_airport

man@the_airport

HOW SOCIAL MEDIA SAVED MY LIFE

One Syrian's Story

HASSAN AL KONTAR

TIDEWATER
PRESS

Published by Tidewater Press
New Westminster, BC, Canada
tidewaterpress.ca

978-1-7770101-8-8 (print)
978-1-7770101-9-5 (e-book)

LIBRARY AND ARCHIVES CANADA CATALOGUING IN PUBLICATION
Title: man@the_airport : how social media saved my life : one Syrian's story / Hassan Al Kontar.
Other titles: Man at the airport
Names: Al Kontar, Hassan, 1981- author.
Identifiers: Canadiana (print) 20210159839 | Canadiana (ebook) 20210160136 | ISBN 9781777010188 (softcover) | ISBN 9781777010195 (HTML)
Subjects: LCSH: Al Kontar, Hassan, 1981- | LCSH: Refugees—Syria—Biography. | LCSH: Refugees—Malaysia—Biography. | LCSH: Internet personalities—Syria—Biography. | LCSH: Social media—Political aspects. | LCSH: Syria—History—Civil War, 2011—Refugees—Biography. | LCSH: Kuala Lumpur International Airport. | LCGFT: Autobiographies.
Classification: LCC HV640.5.S97 A42 2021 | DDC 956.9104/231—dc23

Printed in Canada

This book is made of paper from well-managed FSC® - certified forests, recycled materials, and other controlled sources.

For my parents, Salem and Hoda,
and my family: Solaf, Ammar, Tharaa, Medo and Jasmin.

For my Avenger Team
and all Canadians who welcome refugees.
Canada is more than a place, it is a symbol and an ideal.

And for all Syrians, be they refugees,
prisoners or free men and women.

CONTENTS

FOREWORD

by Nuseir (Nas) Yassin

Palestinian-Israeli Nuseir Yassin is a Harvard graduate who gave up his job to travel the world, making one video a day for a thousand days. Posting his one-minute videos about the people he met and the places he discovered on Facebook as Nas Daily, the vlogger and businessman now has more than 33 million followers across Instagram, Facebook, YouTube and TikTok.

IN MY THOUSAND-DAY journey with Nas Daily, there were only two times when I thought my video was going to kill someone. Literally be the reason they die. One of those two times was in Malaysia, with a Syrian refugee who had been stuck in a Kuala Lumpur airport for six months. He could not enter the country and he couldn't leave it because of passport issues. What happened was that I made a video about him, so that more people could know about his story. I didn't think much about it, but to my surprise the video made an entire government super-angry. And I woke up one day finding myself the reason why that government was putting someone in jail.

That someone was Hassan, and you may have heard of him already because he was all over the news in 2018. Luckily, he didn't die, as you might have realized.

When I first heard about Hassan's story, it was because one of my followers sent me a message on Instagram: "Hey, you should make a video about this guy." They linked me to a news article, where I read this crazy story of a man living in an airport for six months and facing arrest in his own country because he refused to participate in a war. I thought to myself, "Wow, I have to make a video about him."

So I called him up and started chatting with him. To my surprise, Hassan did not sound panicked, worried or tired for someone in his situation. Instead, he was patient, he was funny and, above all, he had a plan. He had been documenting his days in the airport on his personal Instagram, and he knew the uniqueness of his situation would attract attention from journalists and influencers from all around the world. Like Vice, CNN, the BBC. Like me. And he was putting a bet that all this attention on social media would lead to freedom.

Here's the thing. Social media is a powerful tool. To me, as someone who makes videos for a living, it can save a life. Normally we look at social media as a stupid thing: For stupid dances or for stupid challenges and there's nothing much you can gain out of it. That's the perception of social media and the so-called "influencers." But that's not all it can do. When you put social media to good use, it can literally change lives. Because of how easy it is to access anytime, anywhere, it's giving a platform for voices that are not normally covered in the mainstream media. And when something goes viral with millions or billions of views, it's impossible to ignore. What's put on social media can reach governments, policymakers and literally change lives. It's incredible how powerful this machine of social media is.

So that was the basis of Hassan's plan. It was a really crazy, risky plan, but it was a really smart plan, in retrospect. Hassan is the Social Media Refugee, as I like to call him.

After my chat with Hassan, I decided to help him and pulled off a crazy stunt—something that to this day still feels to me a bit like out of a James Bond movie. I couldn't go to Malaysia, so I sent my team to the Malaysian airport, met Hassan, filmed his story entirely in secret and flew back to Singapore, all while avoiding the authorities. We edited the video, published it, and I watched as Hassan's plan worked right before my eyes. I watched as the view count shot up to about eighteen million views—essentially reaching a lot of people in the world.

But here's the catch—his story caught the attention of the good guys, but also the bad guys. Hassan paid the price for his plan. Because he was talking to the media, he got arrested. After the launch of the video, he disappeared. Went completely offline. Nobody knew where he was, and I got scared. He could have been deported to Syria and killed.

Luckily, it all worked out. Because of all the media attention, from Vice, CNN, the BBC and the rest of the world, it reached the Canadian government. When Hassan entered prison, the Canadian government took notice and expedited his application for refugee status. What supposedly would take two years, for Hassan took only two months. He was released, welcomed by his sponsors in Whistler, and he is now enjoying a new life in Canada as a free man. After all he went through, the Social Media Refugee finally got the happy ending he deserved.

But my involvement with Hassan at the airport prison was just a tiny part of his incredible journey from Syria, to the UAE, to Malaysia, to (almost) Ecuador and Cambodia, and back to Malaysia again. And even though everyone knows about the airport prisoner, I'm glad that Hassan has finally decided to share the rest, because it might be even more interesting than the airport prison itself.

That's one minute. See you tomorrow.

INTRODUCTION

SIX MONTHS AFTER I arrived in Canada, I was invited to speak at the Canadian Council for Refugees Spring Consultation in Victoria, BC. It was a sunny day, but the wind was chilly, the kind of breeze that makes you want to spend ten more minutes under the blankets before you get out of bed. I was on the ferry and pulled out my cellphone to take some photos. I loved how Whistler was in the mountains, and still only an hour from the open ocean. I couldn't believe how far I'd come—life was strange, weird, unfair and generous all at the same time. Only a few months before, I'd been in a crowded detention cell in Malaysia, and now I was having poutine on a ferry. In Canada! In the country that every refugee dreams of. Why me? I smiled as I looked at the snow on the distant peaks. I wish my family were here to see this beauty, I thought. I wish they could feel what I am feeling now: safe, legal, hopeful and, yes, finally happy.

The three-day conference was entitled "Roots: Reconciling the global with the local," and one of the other speakers was Carey Newman, a Kwagiulth and Coast Salish artist and a professor at the University of Victoria. It was the first time I'd met and had the chance to listen to a First Nations person. Professor Newman went to the podium and took the mic, but before he started his speech, he began with what sounded like a prayer. He called on his ancestors so their souls could be present and join us, he called on their wisdom and bravery, he called on their history so it could not be forgotten.

Carey was reminding us of all of the suffering his people had faced in a calm, peaceful, musical and painful way.

I was on a chair in the audience when this happened, holding my cup of coffee. I put it down on the floor, took off my glasses and placed them on my knee. I loosened my new tie a little and chewed the inside of my lower lip, something I do when an idea hits me hard and I can't stop thinking about it. Three scenes came into my mind when I closed my eyes: the New Zealand Maori and their haka dance; here, with the prayer of the Indigenous people of Canada; and the long nights filled with stories next to the stove in my village. All three were connected somehow in my mind.

Carey began his speech and was showing some photos, but I could not move. I opened my eyes for a second to have a look at what he was presenting, then closed them again. I did not want to lose the connection I felt at that moment; I did not want to forget what was in my mind. I shook my head and thought, Yes, it's one human civilization we have, not many. And we are not in conflict, even as powers try to convince us we are. We are all connected with each other as human beings, whether we are aware of it or not. We have so much in common: our behaviour and our traditions. I whispered to myself, Only one, only one. Only one human civilization: east, north, south, west, it doesn't matter; different cultures, we are all human.

As I listened to Carey's speech, I thought, we Syrians sing too. We sing war songs, even at our wedding parties, and in these songs we name our ancestors too. The same way the Indigenous people do, not to call their souls but to remember their deeds. And we dance the same way the Maori do in New Zealand—no scary faces, but clapping our hands firmly and calling out with very loud voices.

It was the first day of the conference, and although I was scheduled to be the closing speaker on the third day, I had my speech all ready. But when I went back to my room, I pulled out my notes and added this: Sir, I heard your prayer, and I feel that you and I, we are similar to each other! We also have been forced by circumstances to leave our land and the people we love behind, and no matter how much joy or success we have in our new home, we will always feel the pain of loss. Thank you for accepting us into your land, thank you for your forgiveness.

Current happiness and success, past pain and loss—in my mind these are all connected. I can't separate my childhood, the care my parents gave me, the way they treated me and educated me and the strong relations I have with my siblings from the battles I have been forced to be in and the difficulties I have faced. While I was not a refugee at a camp in Turkey, fleeing from the war in my country, I cannot separate my experience from that of others seeking safety and asylum, be it from Syria or Burma or Somalia or Afghanistan. I cannot separate what it means to be a Syrian from being a new Canadian. When it was my turn to speak, I stood up and said, "Ladies and gentlemen, my name is Hassan Al Kontar. I am a proud Syrian and I am a proud future Canadian."

So, to begin

Now that I was safe, after eight years, I needed to tell my story, but how? Beginnings are hard and become harder as you age, and I was now almost thirty-eight years old. Should I hit the speaking circuit, sharing my "wisdom" with the audience? Someone once sent me a link to a video of a motivational speaker who said, "If you fall, fall forwards." I imagined myself saying to him, That sounds great, buddy, but can you please tell me what difference it makes? A fall is a fall—forward, backward, it doesn't matter. The only thing that matters is that it's okay to fall. They make saying "Give it 110 percent" sound amazing, but I want to ask them, How exactly? There is only a hundred in 100 percent.

So, I needed to write a book. But how should I go from 140

characters to thousands of words? I don't sound or behave like a writer. I always imagine them with messy hair, long beards, oblivious to their appearance because they understand life differently than most of us. I imagine them glancing around rooms checking for details, smoking a lot and, of course, drinking their favourite whisky. They use big words that no one can understand, yet you feel the music in them.

Still, how hard could it be? (It turned out to be very, very hard.) I needed to come up with a plan, so I promised myself that every day I would write for an hour before I went to work and one hour before I went to sleep. For the next two weeks I kept telling myself, Tomorrow, I am going to start. But I didn't.

Then I met a writer, sort of. One cold, sunny Thursday, I was working at the Scandinave Spa in Whistler, a beautiful place—warm inside, charming view, surrounded by mountains and trees, quiet with the kind of music they play in yoga classes. A woman— mid-fifties, thin, tall, salt and pepper hair—came in and ordered an Americano. She chose a table next to the fire, took out two books, some blank paper and a pen and start writing. Just before I called out her order, she closed her eyes and started what looked like a dream, moving her head left and right, up and down. She looks like a writer, I told myself. Either she is imagining the characters or trying really hard to sleep.

I did not want to interrupt her, so I quietly placed the coffee on her table. She continued to hold her pen but wrote nothing. Three minutes later, she opened her eyes, grabbed her things and left without drinking even a sip. That's weird, I thought, but she is a writer, and this is what they do.

Business was slow, so I took a sip of her coffee, opened a Word file on the office PC and wrote, "Beginnings are hard . . ."

Where should I start? My time in the airport, my time in jail? Maybe I needed to start with my family and where I came from—

describe my late father, my forever ideal, the way he prepared me mentally and physically as if he knew that life was going to give me a hard time. Or my mother, the only person I know with absolutely no enemies. She too must have known that life was going to be hard, otherwise why did she force me to go to English summer school all those years? How about my younger brother, Ammar, who made a different decision to me? I rarely spoke about him publicly because I was trying to protect him, or maybe I was trying to protect myself from a kind of pain I could not carry. I had the whole world in one hand, and him in the other. When I presented myself in my videos from the airport, delivering "statements with a smile," I had sounded funny and positive. This book needed to be like that.

Before I could come up with a way to start, I heard a voice saying, "Half caf, half decaf, almond milk and extra foam."

That is complicated, sir! I thought. You must be a writer too.

Part One
MAN

Chapter One

The Olive Farm

FOR THOSE OF us who leave our country for a better future, memory stands still. New buildings, towers, roads, and fancy restaurants may have sprung up, but in your mind, the face of your city remains always the same. If you are no longer there to witness the changes, then you can't imagine them happening, just as you can't imagine that the people you knew can change as well. After years away, you hardly notice the way you've erased all the negatives from your memory, and how your home country has become an ideal—the most beautiful place on Earth. Friends and family may tell you what's new, what's different, but your mind? Well, it just will not absorb it. Later, you will wonder if it is a bad thing to keep the idealized home in your mind untouched, frozen in time.

For most of us, war is something you read about in history books, watch in movies or documentaries. It's not something that happens in your home, to the people you love. If you were a Syrian living abroad in 2011, you changed the TV channel every minute, with the false hope that someone would suddenly say it had all stopped.

Children, their eyes lost and confused, running terrified with their toys in their hands, refusing to forget their innocence in the midst of destruction. Mothers crying with their hands open towards the sky, trying to save those they love and stop the madness; fathers who knew that the normal circle of life is for their children to bury them. But not in Syria, not anymore: wives losing their husbands, coffins on shoulders, rockets and houses falling, tanks moving into cities and terrorists blowing themselves up in the middle of civilian areas. Kidnappers, murderers and rapists everywhere.

The army that I had naively thought belonged to the country turned out to be dedicated to protecting its own interests and those of its leader. On the other side are young men who tasted the sweetness of shooting a weapon and the addiction of the fight. Anger became the master and revenge ruled the streets. I had a wild desire to shout at all of them, "Stop, just stop! We can fix this, we can solve it." Later, I kept quiet because both sides were ready to attack me for not believing in their solution. I told myself, these are not the people I left five years ago. This is not my country. But we were marching into the dark, and no one would be able to stop us.

I, like all Syrians, had to make a decision, a life and death decision that would change my life forever. No one is ever ready for such a decision. It's not the kind you are used to making—renting a new place, changing jobs, buying a car, having the courage to ask that beautiful woman to be your girlfriend. My life, future and destiny lay in the hands of strangers desperately trying to remain in power. Depending on which side I supported, I would be brave or a coward, a patriot or a traitor.

I needed to ask myself the right questions, the difficult ones, the ones no one can ever agree on. Who is right and who is wrong? On which side should I fight and why? Do I need to go back? If so, what about my future? What about my family? Am I the type of man who will have no problem carrying a gun and shooting someone in the name of freedom, or to protect the regime of a corrupt dictator? Who would I be protecting and who would I have to attack? Night after sleepless night, I confronted the reality of this war and what it meant for me, knowing that whatever I decided, I was going to pay for it.

It was our olive farm that finally made up my mind.

Sweida, where I was born and raised, is a small city of half a million inhabitants, a hundred kilometres south of Damascus in a mountainous area. Everyone knows everyone, and it's very social: hunting, playing cards or watching soccer games. Government employees during the week are farmers at the weekends. Time is not very important there, there is no rush. If you miss your bus because you're chatting with an old friend, you can always catch the next one. They even have a saying for that: "Take it easy, it's not like you missed your meeting with the minister." The area is known for growing apples and grapes in the mountains and olives in the plains.

The farm was between our town and the next one, surrounded by other olive farms owned by relatives and delineated by hand-built walls of black stones that gave the place a timeless air. A grapevine grew along one wall, guarding the rows of olive trees. In one corner some almond trees added a garden touch. A small building, two rooms and a terrace, sat atop a hill overlooking the whole farm. We used one of the rooms to store equipment and the other to avoid the midday heat. There was no electricity, but a small generator powered a water pump and, on the rare occasion we decided to stay the night, we attached a lamp to the car battery.

The town dates from the Roman Empire and, if you listen carefully, you could hear the voices of those who once walked and lived there. My grandfather's house, which is still inhabited by one of my father's uncles, is ancient, full of small halls and built of natural black volcanic rock that cools the temperature during the summer. For the winter, there is an old stove that burns dried animal manure instead of wood, an old innovation based on the abundance of cattle and the absence of forest. During the long winter nights, villagers use their stoves to boil wheat. They add sugar and eat it while retelling stories and poems, mostly about our battles against Ibrahim Pasha, son of the great Muhammad Ali, ruler of Egypt at the time of the Ottoman Empire, and against the French General Michaud in 1925. The memories of how we defeated them and kept both our land and our dignity are a part of our DNA and our stories include even the smallest details, down to the individual names of those who fought generations before. We are Druze, a minority in Syria (only three percent of the population); throughout our history we have encountered many attacks, wars and reconciliations based on our beliefs. This is why, in all the countries where we exist (Syria, Israel, Palestine, Jordan and Lebanon), we live in the mountains, where the higher ground gives us isolation and protection, the better to defend ourselves. Although we never fought for power, we have been a major player in the history of Syria.

My city has a history of resisting occupation and, even during our wedding celebrations, we sing to what we call our time of glory, our legacy. Historically rebels who adore freedom, we could not cope with the changing regimes who took control of the Syrian throne, so from the turn of the last century, we started travelling, mostly to Latin America, particularly Venezuela. Almost every family in Sweida has some cousins living there and in other Latin American countries. I myself have many cousins there whom I have never met.

The second wave of emigration came when the previous Syrian president came to power in 1970. He imprisoned some well-known politicians from Sweida and killed others. Knowing our freedoms were going to be taken away from us again, many Druze began to leave and, since the Gulf states were newborn with oil and money, close to home too, we started leaving for there.

If it is true that the man is the son of his environment, then the people who live in Sweida are shaped by land that, despite the olive farms and some seasonal crops, is barren—an endless horizon of medium-sized black rock hills full of caves housing hyenas, wolves, snakes and scorpions, dotted with wild pistachio trees dating back to Roman times. The people there are serious people who don't joke, not with strangers anyway, who stand with each other in time of need, knowing their survival depends on being together. They may have their squabbles but, in the face of an external threat, they become one, and words like dignity, honour, pride and generosity mean everything.

If you, a tourist or explorer coming from a western country, were by chance to visit our town, you would meet simple people with simple needs leading a simple life—smiling, calm, hospitable people, fairly well educated, who would welcome you any time, day or night, and insist that you eat with them. "You can stay as long as you want, the last bus for the city leaves the station by 5:00 p.m. and there is no cellular service." If you got closer, if you stayed longer and they let you in, if you set aside your preconceived ideas of the mysteries of the East—magic nights in the desert, riding camels guided by the stars, living in tents, looking after sheep—you would start to see them differently, and you might realize that this was the problem with every invader who tried to rule this land. They made no effort to understand these people.

So, if you had the chance to have a closer look, you would discover this—they know their land, they are the masters there. They don't attack, but protecting their land and their women is their definition of masculinity. If that were to fail, they could no longer exist, their life would have lost its purpose. Sharply clever by nature, they are generous men of few words, but that all can change in a second. If you come seeking protection, they will protect you no matter what. But if you come as an invader, the volcano that shaped their land thousands of years ago will suddenly erupt. Anger becomes madness—they will be willing to burn themselves down as long as you burn along with them.

The middle class, the majority of this society, provides the community with agricultural products and traditional industries, along with intellectuals, doctors, engineers, officers and skilled workers. This is a community that understands that education is its best and only weapon. They are the writers, poets, artists and athletes. They are the ones who dream of a better country, freedom and democracy, with no corruption. They would be the ones who started protesting, armed with songs from their wedding parties and the principles of their ancestors.

We used to go to the farm every weekend during the summer, and I was not a huge fan. It was hard work, physically demanding—far from the city, friends and TV—and so quiet it was scary. But it was enough for us that my father loved it, a hobby among many, so we went with him, and during the olive harvest the whole family, including my mother and older sister, Solaf, would work. Over time, I started to understand why my father took us with him—so we could know the value of the land and the trees, and that there is happiness in labour and being productive. But mostly he wanted to remind us of our heritage.

One typical summer weekend when I was in Grade Seven, my father and I were having our break under the shadow of an olive tree. The sunlight penetrated the shade through the leaves, a breeze was moving the twigs, and I was trying to sway with it to avoid the heat. Behind us, a hose nourished the same tree, well water so cold and fresh it seemed to come directly from heaven, hitting the red soil with a sound like a small fountain, turning it into something that looked like chocolate and sending a distinctive smell in the air. It sticks with me to this day, the sound of the water and the smell of the soil after rain.

In front of us lay our breakfast, a simple meal of olives, black and green, thyme with olive oil, yogurt, flatbread, cucumber, green onion, green mint, tomato and extra-sweet tea, the way the farmers prefer it, the sugar giving them the energy to continue working. Because I was never a fan of tea or sugar, I was pretending to drink just to fit in.

Without any introduction, my father put down his tea glass, took a quick look around, smiling at the trees, then turned to me and said, "I grew you both together, you know, you and the trees. They are almost your age. Don't let them die thirsty! Add some more rooms to the house, furnish it appropriately, install electricity, plant the remaining land and, no matter what happens, don't sell the farm. It is your and your kids' connection to this village, to your roots."

I still don't know why he picked that day, long before the war started, to remind me of my legacy. But I could feel the presence of history, smell it all over the place, and I looked at him with my eyes narrowed, so he would be able to tell how serious I was and that I understood him. I said just a few words, but it was enough for him to let me drive the car almost two kilometres back to the village as a reward. I think he was looking for some kind of reassurance, to make sure that his message had been heard. What I had said to him was, "If they gave me the weight of this farm in gold, I would not sell it."

Chapter Two

Leaving Syria

I STUDIED LAW at Damascus University; it was what my father wanted me to do. He was a public figure in our city, very involved in politics, and that is what he wanted for me, he believed that was my future. He had come to the conclusion that the best politicians were lawyers, so that was what I was going to be.

Something you should know about us Syrians—we breathe politics. It's in our blood, and if we are doing anything or nothing, we will be talking politics: at our work, during breaks, at dinner parties, the minute we wake up and before we go to sleep, politics. We can't discuss internal politics—red lines drawn by the regime that we'd better not cross if we don't want to disappear—but we discuss foreign politics, near and far, and ordinary people know a great deal about the world. We Syrians also claim to know the answer to any question you may ask, be it how to play iTunes or do open-heart surgery. "No" or "I don't know" is not an acceptable answer for us.

In 1958, during the signing ceremony of the unity agreement between Syria and Egypt, the Syrian president told the Egyptian president, "You don't know what you have taken on, Mr. President. You have joined a people where everyone is political: fifty percent think they are leaders, twenty-five percent think they are prophets, and at least ten percent think they are gods."

My father wanted to put me on the right path, if not as a politician, then as someone who could serve the public and have a great career. We didn't discuss it much. I thought he knew what was best, and I thought I wanted what he wanted for me.

I hated it—genuinely, deeply, passionately hated it. As I laboured through the heavy textbooks, I knew that this was not for me, these dry technical details. This was not how my mind operates. I like ideas, strategies, vision, and I wasn't going to change the world, or try to, by reading about how to prosecute a murderer. What I really wanted to do was write. Journalism was my dream, and I loved articles that explained the reasons behind the deep issues: political, historical and inspirational. But my father was right—Syria, where the media is controlled by the government and intelligence services, was no place for a career in journalism.

What to do with my life? I decided I wanted to be my own man. Young Syrians before the war started were like their peers around the world, something I understood more clearly after I arrived in Whistler and started meeting young people from all over Europe, Australia and New Zealand, who came there for the sake of adventure. We all have that phase in our life when we want to travel the world, make our own decisions and find personal freedom with less control or observation from our families. For Arabs, it's normal to live with your family even when you are an adult and married; we never cut our relationship and connection with our own blood, no matter how far away we live or the last time we saw them. But I was an adult and I wanted to feel like one. I wanted to get on a plane so badly because of what it represented to me: freedom, adulthood and adventure.

Financial independence was something else I craved. I wanted a job with good money to help me build my future, and in Syria I knew there would be no such thing. A number of my friends had travelled to the United Arab Emirates to work, and when they came back on holiday, their stories about Dubai—the wealth, lifestyle, roads, towers, beaches, nightclubs—were enticing. It sounded good and I, like so many others, wanted that. Syrians could get a two-month tourist visa to go to the UAE; if you could find a job, that would be converted to a work visa that would allow you to remain. Everyone I spoke to agreed that to have a good job there, you needed two essential things: English and computer skills. I had both, so I was confident that I would be successful.

The other compelling reason to go to the UAE was Syria's compulsory military service. If you are eighteen years old, not your mother's only male child and if you are no longer a student, you must serve in the military for two years. While I was still at university, I submitted a form annually to show that I was still enrolled and not failing, but that was no longer an option for me. The government wanted two years of my life, my future, and that was something I didn't want to hand over to the regime.

There was one escape. If you were living and working abroad, you could pay money as a substitute for service. As with students, you needed to send a document, stamped by Syrian Embassy officials in the country of your residence, as proof of your exempt status. And the fee, of course—US$3,500 per year. After the war started in 2011 the amount doubled. If you failed to pay the money or to send the annual documentary proof, you would be arrested at the airport the moment you stepped back on Syrian soil. This was and still is the system today.

The closest airport to Sweida is Damascus, around a hundred kilometres away, and going there to welcome someone home was one of our favourite things to do, not just for me and my family, but for all people from my city. With us, it is like a tradition, a joyous road trip in a full, hired bus, all of us singing and making music on the way to the airport. Someone is returning home, happy and excited, and he should come out and see the happy faces of the people he missed and loves. For me, everything related to air travel was an adventure, from the traffic policeman we had to bribe to let us leave the bus in the parking area, to the coffee shop designed to look like an old Damascus house, to the landing on the second floor from where you could watch the takeoffs and landings. I would look closely at the faces of those who were about to travel, especially the foreigners, trying to figure out their thoughts, their language and the kind of life they had. When I was back home, I could look up at the sky and remember the faces of those whom I just met at the airport, the memories bringing me one step closer to finding all the answers to the questions I used to ask myself on my balcony.

It was March 23, 2006, when I first saw Damascus Airport through the eyes of a traveller. Now it is me, I am actually going to see it from the inside this time, I told myself, sparkling with excitement. I was twenty-five years old, and about to explore shops, restaurants and duty-free. I was going to be checked with a metal detector and security scanned, pushing my trolley with my passport and mobile in my hand, the way travellers carry it. I was going to stand at the gate and board the plane this time—this was huge! After years of watching and wondering, I was about to experience it all, and when I did, it did not disappoint me (except for the argument with the flight attendant who wouldn't let me drink the beer I had bought from the duty-free). It was exactly as I had dreamed: to cross the line between daylight and darkness, to see clouds from inside, to be higher than any bird.

Abu Dhabi was my destination, the capital of the United Arab Emirates, two hours and forty-five minutes from Damascus. Hugging my family to say goodbye for the first time was something I will never forget: my mother's hands on my face, warm and full of tenderness, rubbing my beard; my father's question, "What am I going to do now without you?"

It was both my choice and a necessity. I needed to find the answers. I needed to discover them myself, to build a different future, one we can't have in Syria. I wanted to walk through in reality those photos and movies of the outside world I used to watch. With the cousins and many friends I had in the UAE, it would be an adventure, but not that big a change for me. That was what I thought.

Chapter Three

Two Faces

YOU CAN SMELL the money. It's the first thing you notice, having left Damascus and taken your first step in Abu Dhabi airport. So much wealth, such a culture shock—it frightened me. We have thousands of years of civilization in Syria, but we don't have the modern technology and material goods. The only two new Mercedes cars in Sweida were owned by senior government officials: the provincial governor and the senior Ba'ath Party official. All the other Mercedes cars were old, from the fifties and sixties, and we used them as taxis. But in UAE, they were everywhere, beginning with a display at the airport lounge.

I had to pause there, trying to absorb it all—the huge hall with the emerald-coloured column rising from the floor and fanning out across the ceiling far above my head surrounded by fancy restaurants, luxury shops and designer clothes. There seemed to be cameras everywhere, and people were speaking Arabic with a different accent, one I had only heard on TV. The air conditioning was strange and unfamiliar, cold, but not the fresh cold I was used to at home. As I stood there, like a little kid who has just lost his mother in the mall, I realized I had been excited about the plane trip, but hadn't really looked ahead to the reality of this. Big questions roamed in my head: What is going to happen? Will I be able to find a job in this country? What should I do now? Everyone seemed to be in a rush, to know where they were heading, busy checking their cellphones. With the old Arabic proverb, "He who asks will never get lost" in my head and with my tourism visa in my hand, I went through immigration, where officials scanned my retina and stamped my passport. Outside the air was very hot and disturbing. I called my family to tell them that I had arrived, that I was okay.

I could live with cousins from my father's side for a short time but the pressure to find a job began on the first day. I soon discovered that having some English, computer skills and a driving licence didn't count for anything without some local experience. My one-page resume (typed up with big fonts to make it look full and impressive) winged its way to every company with a vacancy on its website that I could find at the internet café. Walking back to my uncle's house, I'd buy newspapers solely for the job advertisements. Some calls came, and a few interviews, but no offers of employment. During those weeks, I tried my best not to behave as if I was on holiday—I was a job-seeker, not a tourist. I didn't visit the towering buildings, learn the street names, or go to malls or beaches; I did not want to get attached to a country I might not be able to stay in.

My father was a distant but daily presence, calling me to check if there were any updates, noting my confusion and stress but offering up nothing but a smile. It was as if he were setting a test for me. At the time, I didn't know why. To make me stronger? I could imagine him giving me his "look," the one that could make all of us—Solaf, Ammar, the cousins—cower. Moving his glasses to the tip of his nose, he'd look over them at you, raising one eyebrow and narrowing the other eye, letting you know he was a man to be respected and obeyed. As the deputy director of a civil service department, he was well connected and highly regarded. Cultured, clever and a disciplinarian, he could be both firm and kind, and nothing was more important to him than his kids. So after six weeks of me trying and failing to find a job, and with only fifteen days left on my visa, he finally called.

"Write down this phone number. He is my friend and owns a big group of companies in Sharjah, next to Dubai. Call him, tell him who you are, go and meet him. He will give you a job and a free work permit, a different permit to the usual one, a better one. It will allow you to leave anytime you find a better job without the current employer's approval. Take care of yourself."

As simple as that! After a month and a half of being worried, my father solved my problem in a one-minute call.

My father's friend was the owner of the third biggest group of companies in Sharjah, with thousands of employees, and I was about to become one of them. For my interview, I wore a tie and was foolishly confident. Two secretaries escorted me to his office, which took up more than half of the second floor. His desk was on a dais and behind it, his chair was like a throne. He was a small man in that big chair, and he spoke gently and kindly, smiling with the assurance that money and power give. I handed him my resume, which I immediately regretted when he glanced at it briefly, smiled and put it aside.

"Your father wants you to be in the spare parts division. That is something to be expected from the son of a mechanical engineer who has great experience. You know, I asked your father to come and work here, with me. That is an offer I never give to anyone, but he refused."

I saw an opportunity to impress him. "Now you have his son, sir."

"Yes, I do," he laughed. "It will be enough for me if you are half as good as he is."

It turned out I was nowhere near half as good.

My unwillingness to show interest in anything mechanical always bothered my father, as did my avoidance of math, his favourite subject. He passed some of his passion on to Ammar, but not to me. When we were fixing the water pump at our farm, my father desperately tried to get me engaged, explaining what he was doing, what the problem was and how to fix it. But the only answer I was interested in was, "Is it going to take long? Are we done yet?" I was more like my mother, in love with history, not machinery, with words and novels, not toolboxes.

My interview with the manager of the spare parts department did not take long. He asked me to identify various bits of silver metal arranged on the shelves. True to the Syrian habit of claiming we know everything, I threw out names, trying to remember what my father might have called them. When asked to explain how the engine works, I launched into a flight of imagination. It was embarrassing and humiliating, and I just wanted to run out of the spare parts department. Thirty minutes later, my father called.

"What in God's name did you just invent?"

"I invented nothing. I just simply and clearly explained how the engine works from my point of view."

"Your point of view? Science can't explain that."

"Yet!"

"Don't be a smartass. Working in spare parts is good money. Anyway, they've decided you're going to work in the insurance department. Miss you. Good luck."

Insurance clerk. That was my title, and my new office was one room with four desks, two computers, three filing cabinets and two bosses. My excitement and happiness at finding a job disappeared and was replaced by disappointment.

When I asked to whom I should report, both said at the same time, "To me." Two managers in one department may sound strange, but not for this part of the world, I would learn. There is the actual manager who does the managing, who studies the cases and makes the decisions. Then there is the manager who just signs the paperwork. One has his title because of what he knows, his expertise; the other (annoying) one is there because of who he knows, his personal connections. The Al Marwan insurance department was my first experience of how some people enjoy using the limited power they have to intimidate others. It's like a drug that makes them feel more important and gives them their purpose. It is respect by fear and it is built into the system. It was also the first time I experienced selfless generosity and genuine kindness from someone not in my family.

Our working day was divided into two shifts, from 8:00 a.m. to 1:00 p.m., then from 4:00 until 8:00, six days a week. Because where I was staying was some distance away and the traffic was bad, I soon decided not to go home during the midday break. I would stay at work with my two managers, eat something, read a book and sleep a little on my desk.

Mr. Khwajah, from Pakistan, was in his mid-sixties He was the actual manager. After nineteen years working as a bank manager, he had found himself with no job at the age of sixty; because UAE law does not permit foreigners to have citizenship or permanent residency no matter how many years you've spent serving and helping them build their country, Mr. Khwajah had had to take the position in my insurance department.

Mr. Khwajah taught me about insurance and helped me with my English. He loved the language of Shakespeare and spoke like a character from an English novel—the only thing missing was a pipe and high tea. It could be confusing, and sometimes employees from the insurance companies we dealt with would call me up to double-check what it was exactly that he wanted. "We'll pay the claim, but can you please ask him to speak *our* kind of English?"

Mr. Khwajah also loved food. At lunch, I would ask, "Would you like to have shawarma today, sir?"

"Yes, please."

"Which one? Chicken or meat?"

He would think deeply for a long moment, then, "Both."

With time, he began inviting me to his home, and we became very close. One morning, he came to the office, sat, asked for his tea with milk, and handed me a stack of three books topped with a document headed with, "In the name of Her Majesty The Queen" and then my name. He said nothing, waiting. He knew me and I couldn't disappoint him.

"Her Majesty The Queen? Lovely lady, I've seen her on the TV once or twice, but I did not know we were friends. Did her husband, the Duke of Edinburgh, know she was writing to me? What does she want anyway? Insurance for her car? Or for one of her racehorses?"

He covered his face with his hands, shaking his head.

"You are now enrolled in the CII. I paid the fee, and your exam for a certificate in insurance is in three months. Study those books."

"CII? Fees? Exam? What are you speaking about, dear Mr. Khwajah?"

"It is the Chartered Insurance Institute, accredited internationally and the most important insurance education centre in the world."

I was stunned. No more was he the English lord who lost his pipe. He sounded, looked and acted like a father. I began to understand how a relationship can be built, and what it means to create trust and love between two men forty years apart in age, from different countries with different customs and languages. What I didn't know at the time was how much it had cost—the equivalent of six months of my salary—and Mr. Khwajah had paid it knowing I would not be able to pay him back. Logic doesn't explain why some people act the way they do; the actions of the heart are different from the actions of the mind and it's not necessary to analyze the reasons behind them. I walked to him and hugged him.

"Why, sir?"

"Because I love you and want the best for you. And because I believe in you."

That was dear Mr. Khwajah, as I always called him, the man with the double shawarmas, chicken and beef.

Mr. George was my other manager, a Syrian like me, and the complete opposite of Mr. Khwajah. He was in his mid-fifties, spoke very little English and wore a gold bracelet around his right wrist that drove me mad—it seemed to be the epitome of all he was, bossy and exploitative. He never missed a chance to use all office resources for his private work and was always lecturing us about modern management techniques. But I still had to mark up all the correspondence with a pencil to show him where he had to sign.

Three months after I started, Mr. George decided to fire the fourth member of our department, the driver. He was another Syrian, twenty-five years old and married with one child. He had some education, not cultured or sophisticated, but he was a man with a good heart who was trying to support his family. His mistake had been to make a joke that he was a personal employee at Mr. George's company, not Al Marwan.

Because the owner of the company himself had hired me, I was protected from Mr. George. I discovered my salary was less than that of similarly ranked colleagues in the accounts and HR department, but it didn't bother me. What I needed was experience, the time to learn and improve, to get to know how the system worked and to build a personal network.

The United Arab Emirates is a newborn country, only ten years older than I am, founded in 1971. Whenever I told this fascinating fact to someone, the reply would usually be, "And yet, look how far they have come with all this progress." That was true, but for me, progress meant something else, something related to history, identity and civilization.

After two years with Al Marwan, I took a new job, also in insurance, in Dubai. The city was too expensive for me to live in so, like most people in middle management, I commuted each day from Sharjah. Soon after I started working, a friend and I moved into an apartment downtown, close to where the work bus picked me up every day, and I lived there all the time I worked in Dubai. Sharjah is a big residence hotel for those who work in Dubai, no bars or night clubs allowed as it is ruled by Islamic law, unlike Dubai. So people live there because it's cheaper but have all their fun in Dubai.

Dubai is the leader in both tourism and business. It was and is growing very fast. It is indeed a beautiful city and one tour by car is enough to be impressed—the biggest mall, the tallest tower, the fanciest restaurants, the wildest highways. It is a city whose sun attracts those steeped in rain and snow in their countries. It is designed to serve them and to charm the hearts of those who have money. You will love it if you are a tourist, rich or white. The real Dubai, however, the one no one sees in the media, is where the workers who built all of these towers live. Dubai is a city whose bottom hides a lot of tales, secrets and tragedies.

Every city in this world has two faces, and we normally see and judge them through one of two eyes: the eye of a tourist and the eye of a resident. Tourists discover the adventure, the beaches, the warm sun, the nightclubs and luxury hotels. Residents discover the reality, what's not in the glossy pamphlets. Who built these towers? How much did they get paid? Where do they live? What about their contracts, what rights do they have? What are their working conditions? Where they are from? What are their stories? Foreign workers, looking through our residents' eyes, all know the answers but speaking about them can lead to imprisonment and deportation. The UAE is a modern country with an old system of slavery, or at least indentured servitude.

The workers who come to the UAE in their hundreds of

thousands have one purpose only—to build the cities where the tourists can enjoy themselves. When they finish or once their contract has expired, they leave, no matter how many years they lived there. They don't know the country: they know their rooms, the bus that takes them to work, the blazing heat they work in, the tower they are building, their daily rice meal and the airport when they leave. I don't know what happened to that driver who dared to make a joke.

As Syrians, fellow Arabs, we were in the middle rank of the class structure in the Emirates. At the top of the occupational and social pyramid, you will find the locals, owners and rich people; next to them you will find the white foreigners, from Europe and the USA. Among the locals the conviction is that anyone white with blue eyes must be an expert, and these expatriates normally work as managers and consultants, with huge salaries and the best places to live. But for us, the same rule applies as for the other foreign workers. When I first moved to the Emirates, the fact that I could not become a permanent resident or citizen, that my security was dependent upon an employer and a work visa, was not a concern for me. I was young, employed and not paying too much attention.

My next and last legal job was as the marketing manager for an insurance company in Abu Dhabi. While Dubai has the world-famous reputation, Abu Dhabi is the capital and where the decisions are made: policy, homeland security, intelligence, foreign relations. The two cities seem to be in competition, with a mix of jealousy and inter-dependence. In 2010, I was sitting in a modest local coffee shop in Dubai with a friend. It was the kind of place where locals or Arabs go to smoke hookah, and on that day we were smoking and watching the TV for the opening ceremony of the Burj Dubai (or so we thought it was to be called), the tallest tower in the world. This was a source of pride for the people of Dubai, especially after the financial crisis and the embarrassment of being bailed out by Abu Dhabi. Then it came, the moment no one expected, the moment the name was announced by the ruler of Dubai—not Burj Dubai, as the tower had been called while under construction for the last six years, but Burj Khalifa, after the president and ruler of Abu Dhabi. Silence filled the café. You could hear the locals cursing in their depths without making a sound. Their eyes said everything—they belonged to Abu Dhabi now. In the heat of their anger, they all stood up, forgetting about the television and their hookah, and left.

It was hard for me, like it was hard for most foreigners, to make friends among the locals. In the eleven years I lived there, I had only one, Matar Al Shamsi, my manager at the Al Khazna Insurance Company in Abu Dhabi. It began when he caught me secretly reading during office hours. He asked what the book was and I showed him *The Kingdom* by Robert Lacey. He grabbed my hand, took me to his office, opened up a window on his PC, and there it was, the same book. He was reading it secretly during worktime too. The only difference that I was reading the Arabic version while he was reading the English one.

Fifteen years older than me, married with three kids (two girls and a boy), Matar had studied at university in Miami, which is why he was fluent in English, but what I liked about him the most is what he hated the most—that he was poor. Or at least that is how he saw himself. For reasons I never understood, the only money he had was his and his wife's salary. For me, this was still a huge amount of money, but for the way other locals were accustomed to living, it was nothing. .

"I am suffering!" he used to say. And I would reply, "Yes, you are! It's hard not to have a Mercedes when everyone else has two." He would laugh at this joke, but for him it was not funny. It's hard to be the only sane man in a land of madness when the only cure is to be as crazy as they are.

In Syria, we have a phrase for whenever we come across someone who is not doing well in a foreign country: "It is not meant to be for everyone." Ammar had joined me in the UAE in 2010 but, unlike me, my brother was never happy there. He has this huge, independent, strong personality with lots of dignity, and he was not okay with a labour system where your destiny depends on how much your sponsor is happy with you. He was not okay with another human playing the role of God in control of his life.

In February 2011, Ammar decided to go back to join the army for his mandatory service. Once he finished, he would find work and stay there, next to our parents, that was the plan. Solaf, who now had a three-year-old son, was working as an English teacher in Kuwait, where her husband was an engineer, so my parents were alone in Syria. For us, that was not acceptable. It's a matter of tradition—your parents should not be left alone. What if one of them gets sick? What if they need any kind of physical help? Who is going to help my father on the farm? Who is going to buy and carry the groceries for my mother, and help her move the heavy furniture?

I was worried about Ammar going back, but neither of us could have imagined that one of the most brutal wars in modern history was coming, nor could we have foreseen that the whole world would join the fight. I did not know that I would regret helping him make that decision for the rest of my life. Back in Syria, he joined the army. Fifteen days later, the protests began. I have always felt the responsibility of fatherhood toward Ammar and I was constantly afraid for him.

Dubai, March 2011. I was alone in my room, sitting on the couch with the remote control in one hand, switching from one news channel to another, and my cellphone in the other, trying to get updates, trying to understand what was going on. Dirty coffee cups were scattered on the table in front of me, cigarette butts filled the ashtray, and smoke and the white noise from the air-conditioner filled the room. Hundreds of updates on the screen, hundreds of thoughts in my mind, and no proper food or good sleep for days. I'd ignored the calls from Matar who, as my manager, wanted to know why I hadn't shown up.

I was worried about my parents, my family, Ammar and Syria. No one knew what was going to happen. Would the insurgents be able to remove the regime as we all hoped? How long would it take? Was it going to end soon? No one was sure about anything, and anxiety was eating all of us. Talking with other Syrians in Dubai, we argued about the best solution and what we should do, the correct way to do it, without any of us listening to the others. Then I remembered my father and his story at the farm. I stopped—it felt like I had lost something I was looking for and suddenly found it.

I don't need the foreign news to tell me what is going on in Syria, I told myself. I'm Syrian, it's my country and I know better than they do. I don't need them to tell me what I should do. I know what to do. My father had told me when he said, "Plant, build and don't sell." That was it, the decision was made. I did not exist in this life to uproot trees, but to plant them; not to destroy houses, but to build them; not to sell, but to keep. I did not exist in this life to kill anyone, no matter what. I will not be a part of this war in any form, will not pay the money required to exempt me from military service. If I cannot stop it, I will not be a part of it. As simple as that, I thought at the time.

It was both a logical and sentimental decision, one I knew would cost me a lot, but one that was correct. The protests had just started, blood boiled in my veins, everything was moving quickly. The hopes were so high, and the dream was so big. My people were asking for freedom, democracy, elections, an end to corruption, just like Tunisia and Egypt. The Arab Spring had accomplished this in months, and we thought, naively, that if the movement came to Syria, real reforms would be possible and soon we would be a free country again. I still had a valid passport and I was still working. I could wait a few months to pay my military deferment.

I didn't discuss my decision with my family. It was not a debate and they were in the middle of a war that was escalating quickly. Instead I lied to them about my situation so that they would not worry. They thought I was safe and there was no need for me to come back.

I got my first indication of what was going to happen in Syria, and how long it would take, when I met the General, as Matar referred to his American friend. He had been talking about this friend and business partner for months, about the plans they had to launch a new security training company together. Matar was no different from others in the way he looked at westerners, the blond-man-and-green-eyes complex as my friends and I used to call it. This business partner was a former soldier who had served in Lebanon, Iraq and Afghanistan, and who had published some books that the Pentagon used in their military training programs. The way Matar described him, it was as if he had found a treasure trove and his heart's desire—riches—was close. This man was the way to his dream, and he talked about him as if he were a god, with the halo of a saviour who was going to lead him to absolute victory. I tried to temper his enthusiasm—"You talk about this guy like he is General Colin Powell!"—but didn't want to take his hope and dream away.

There was nothing remarkable about the day I finally met the General, just the routine smell of coffee and the remnants of our lunch on the table next to Matar's desk. No doubt, no sins. It turned out that he wasn't actually a general, but that didn't matter. It also didn't matter that he wasn't blond and his eyes weren't green—Malcolm Nance looked more like Colin Powell than Dwight Eisenhower. I was ready to see him as a hero too, an oracle of wisdom who might have answers for me about the situation in Syria.

Matar tried hard to engage me in their conversation, but although my body was present, my mind was back there, back home. Then something the General said got my attention. I sat up in my chair, opened my eyes and ears, and waited for him to finish without interrupting.

"We had a reception at the American Embassy yesterday, and we were all there," he said. "I had a good time."

"Was the ambassador or the consul present?" I asked

"Yes, they were both there."

I nodded my head and said nothing, but after a while he took the bait. Having exhausted the business talk, he decided to speak about something else, still close to his specialty.

"You told me you are from Syria, right?"

"Yes, that is right."

"From which city?"

"It's called Sweida, in the southern region."

He nodded and made clear he knew the area and was familiar with the geography. "What do you think is going to happen there, and for how long?"

This was a new and different question for me, not the routine question people used to ask: who are you supporting? His question made me think. It looks like he has something to say, I thought, so I decided to play dumb, to feed his ego and give him the chance to lecture me.

"It's hard to tell. I hope it's going to end soon. What do you think?"

"A year. It will take a year," was his answer.

His words fell on me like a bomb. It had only been a few weeks since the protests started, and here was this man, a former soldier and a security expert who had been at a reception the night before with the US ambassador, saying it would last a year. Mr. Nance kept talking but I could not really take anything in. The only thought in my head was, these are not his words, they're someone else's, someone from yesterday's reception. I did not want to believe him, but I went home that day with the certain feeling that the worst was yet to come and that it was going to last a long time.

With the days and months that passed, the General and I became friends. Along with Matar, we would go camping in the desert. Whenever we met, I would look at him, smile and ask, "Did you have any new meetings at the embassy? Is there any news, please?"

And he used to laugh out loud and answer, "You are one of my two favourite people in the UAE."

Two years later, I heard that the security company had failed to get a single contract, and my friend was serving time in jail for late loan payments. Sometimes, I'd see Malcolm Nance on CNN, talking as a security expert about the war in Syria.

By then I was drowning in my own problems. I always knew my decision was correct but that it would cost me a lot, and it did. I had surrendered myself to the desert sands and opened the gates of hell for years to come.

Chapter Four

Between the Camel and the Range Rover

A MONTH AFTER I said goodbye to Ammar, my passport expired. I didn't even try to renew it. I was afraid to show up at the embassy because, since the war had started, rumours were flying around the Syrian community in the UAE. Young men my age and in my situation were telling stories of the embassy refusing to renew the passport of anyone eligible to pay the deferment fee—no money, no passport renewal. There was word of cases where the embassy held onto the passports; if you didn't pay, the Emiratis would send you back to Syria. Either way, the government had you—your money, or your body in the army. My work permit was still valid for another three months or so, and I was optimistic the upheaval in Syria would end as quickly as it had in other countries in the region.

On the day my work permit expired, I was working at Al Khazan's Dubai branch. The Human Resources Manager from the head office in Abu Dhabi called me in for a meeting the same day, and when I arrived he handed me my termination papers. I went home to the apartment I shared in Sharjah unemployed and officially an illegal. For the next five years my life would be a day-to-day existence of uncertainty and insecurity, always knowing that at any moment I could be arrested and deported.

A cousin of mine owned a solar panel business in Dubai, and he offered me an off-grid job working for him. That worked for three or four months, until another cousin wanted my job. The first cousin had never been able to say no to this one, so I was fired from my unofficial job.

A life with no friends around is hard, but losing them is harder. You never stop missing them, and although you are angry at what drove you apart, you never stop hoping that they will return; you are always ready to forgive and forget, if only *they* would make the first move. Male ego and pride stop you from being the one to reach out first.

Majdi and I were inseparable as children, practically growing up together and best friends from Grade Seven. Our friendship continued when we both moved to the UAE, he working and living in a different state, but spending three days a week at my place. He'd make excuses to his manager about expanding their business in my area, but it was just an excuse so we could remain close and spend time together. It was normal for me to come home and find him already in my apartment, showered and takeaway food ordered for our dinner. Then he got married, his wife did not like me much, and that was it. One argument and we stopped speaking to each other.

One morning in 2013, I received one of those wake-up calls that you know means bad news because of the hour. When you recognize the number, hundreds of terrible thoughts cross your mind. Both my father and my mother were on the line, and I could hear them crying. I listened to my father fighting tears, trying to overcome his inability to speak without sobbing. Then I heard him say, "I wish you were here standing next to me. I need you."

The moment those words reached me, I knew that here was something that was going to change our family forever. In our culture men don't cry—it's a sign of weakness—but the greatest grief or greatest happiness can still bring tears.

"What is wrong? What happened?"

"Ismail has passed away."

Solaf, Medo and Ismail had returned to Syria so that Ismail could have open-heart surgery. Now, at the age of forty-five, my brother-in-law was gone, leaving Medo and Solaf alone. While I grieved for Ismail, I was grieving more for the loved ones he'd left behind. For the next week I tried and tried to speak to Solaf, but I only managed to do so once because she was heavily sedated most of the time.

At the time, I was illegal but I still had a place to live. I had come up with half of the first month's rent, enough to sublet an apartment, but then I couldn't pay anything for the next one and half months. I kept coming up with excuses—my family will send me the money, my company is transferring my termination benefits, I found a temporary job. "Tomorrow, or two days, I promise," I kept telling the landlord, even though I had no money and no plan.

Sitting on the edge of my bed that morning, the room still in total darkness, I covered my face with my hands and felt completely powerless and hopeless. I thought about Majdi and said to myself, He will call me now when he hears this news. This is a death, when every other problem becomes as nothing. Now is the time to act like men. I needed him to call, and I waited all that day and the long day after, but his call never came. I never saw him again, and learned it is especially painful to love someone who will never love you back, or to wait for someone who will never come.

The landlord finally asked me to write a cheque so he could go to the police if I failed to pay. I refused, so he kicked me out. Now, in addition to being weak, afraid, lonely and lost, I was homeless. The sun was blazing as I pulled my two suitcases behind me along the sidewalk, heading to the nearest mall, looking for refuge from the heat. What next? Where would I go now? I wouldn't be able to stay in the mall forever. I couldn't walk around the streets with two suitcases—the police might stop me. It was both dangerous and dispiriting.

The cold air-conditioned air inside the mall was the difference between hell and heaven. They should put up a statue to the man who invented this, I thought (after more than six years in the UAE I felt differently about air conditioning than I had when I first arrived at Abu Dhabi Airport). I scanned the small signs hanging from the ceiling: fire exit, stairs, food hall—no, not those—I was looking for a toilet sign so I could wash my face and dry my sweaty clothes to look like a genuine shopper. It was around 10:00 a.m. and people were sitting at the coffee bars and strolling through the shops: Armani, Dolce & Gabbana, Louis Vuitton. It was surreal and incomprehensible and upsetting to watch the happy faces of the shoppers and try to figure out their stories and habits, having cleaned myself up in public toilets. I didn't know it at the time, but it was a sample of what was going to be my future.

After several hours, I decided to call Jehad. Like Majdi, Jehad had lived in our neighbourhood at home and we'd known each other since we were three years old. He had also ended up in the Emirates and was now married to Donia, a great woman, with two children. He lived in a different state, but we'd stayed close. He remains my only friend from the old days in Syria and the newer days in the UAE.

"What are you doing?" I asked him. I could feel the numbness in my feet, after walking around the mall for most of the day, and with no food, not even a cup of coffee. My creativity was limited.

"Donia and I are visiting some friends. What's going on with you?"

He knew I was not okay, but this is how we always started our conversations, chat about work, health, family.

"I have a problem."

"Where are you now?"

"Nowhere. With my suitcases."

"I am coming."

The UAE is a small country—you can drive from one end to the other in three and a half hours if there isn't any traffic, but there is always traffic. It took Jehad two hours to reach me from his home in Al Ain. The first thing I said to him when he found me was, "Can you buy me a coffee, please?"

For the two-hour return trip, he didn't talk, didn't question me. He played some music while I looked out the window until we reached his home—he knew I'd had enough. After a shower, I slept like one of his children, feeling temporarily safe. I stayed there for a few days, while he helped me find another place in Abu Dhabi, the city that would witness the last chapter of my life in the UAE.

The first few months in Abu Dhabi were kind of a break for me, a time to catch my breath. I stayed with a friend for a while until I managed to find off-grid work at a new motor oil company by telling them I had a valid work permit from my previous employer. They didn't mind at first, as work permits cost a lot and they were a start-up. I worked as their sales and marketing manager for several months, giving the company a strong start and participating in important exhibitions. They liked me and my work and wanted me to transfer my permit to them so I wouldn't be able to leave. I stalled for a while, but when they asked for a copy I had to tell them the truth. They couldn't keep me as it was a huge risk and a big fine if we were caught. They had to let me go and I was homeless once again.

I started living here and there and anywhere—public gardens, stairways—walking around, resting and cleaning myself in mosques, and slowly maxing out my credit cards. What do I do now? was the question I asked myself. Most people who work off-grid are carpenters, plumbers or electricians from Asia, Bangladesh, Pakistan or India who work until they have a good amount of money then turn themselves into immigration, get a ticket and go back home. I had no experience in these things and a job like that would be high risk; those who hire you know that you can't go to the police or labour office to complain.

I'd gained some experience in the solar panel business working at my cousin's company, so I decided to promote myself as a freelance installer. Until that time, I had used Facebook to connect with family and friends, but I knew that Instagram was the most popular social media platform in the UAE. That was where I needed to promote myself. I set up a profile on Instagram, using "UAE Solar Freelance Installer," a fake profile photo and images of solar panels I'd grabbed from the internet. My profile description said, "Install, maintain, design solar stations to generate electricity."

It worked. I managed to get a small installation and maintenance project because of my new Instagram profile. It was perfect: easy, small, quick and good money. The problem was I had no car to get there. I reached out to a former customer, a young Yemeni who worked in a car rental office in Abu Dhabi. I was the one who used to issue the insurance policies for their cars. In his late twenties, he had a good heart and minimal personal hygiene, which made two of us at that point. I explained the situation and promised to give him a share of my wages if he rented a car under his name. He accepted, I did the job and gave him his money, offering to keep our arrangement going. Now I had a temporary home—a white Hyundai Sonata sedan, new, clean, with power windows, remote control, dark fabric seats, a good sound system and a plastic dashboard with blue lights that was beautiful at night. For the first few days, I felt happy to be able to move around and enjoy the cold air from the air conditioner in the hot summer.

To be honest, I had no idea what I was doing in the beginning, but with the help of Google and common sense, I start installing solar panel stations. I wasn't very successful, as potential customers would contact me and ask to come to my office. "I can bring my office to you! My car is my office." I thought it was funny, and funny might save the day, but in most cases I never heard back from them. Fortunately, the guy who rented me the car was patient. He had lots of cars and rarely ran out of them, so he didn't actually need mine. Whenever I got a job, I would pay him and the rental fee. Sometimes it took months, but I always paid.

If I wasn't working and had some gas, I would drive around, listen to some music and park here and there. If I had no money, I would park and walk into the mosque, a small two-storey one, new and well designed with an air conditioner and cold water. I would go upstairs, lean back against the wall and try to relax or take a nap between prayers.

Nights were the worst. I couldn't keep the engine running to get some cold air; a running car in the same spot would bring too much attention. I could not keep the windows down because it's even more hot and humid that way, and I could not drive around as there were more police at night. So I know how hell smells and what it feels like—it's a closed car on a summer night in Abu Dhabi with a human being inside it. When, swimming in my own sweat, I couldn't take it anymore, I would run the engine for five minutes for some cold air, re-doing it again and again.

That was the process every single night during the summertime. Once, when I had no gas and couldn't take it anymore, I went to the mosque. Even though it was closed, the cold water was outside and I put my head under the tap, furious but with nowhere to direct my anger. I discovered that, even though the mosque was closed, the air conditioner inside was still running, and the small crack between the floor and door leaked cold air. I lay down and started flipping myself over every once in a while, just to feel the cold air.

During the years that followed, the years of hiding, avoiding eye contact and conversations with almost everyone, I introduced myself to fishing. Before, I had always thought it a boring hobby, with nothing but waiting and wasting time, but I was wrong. There is a different angle, a wider and deeper one, a way to help you understand the secret behind it. As I had no home to go to, I spent my nights fishing, which became my recreation. For a long time, fishing was my favourite activity, one that allowed me to escape from my problems and from reality, to clear my head and think of nothing but listen to music, watch and hear the waves, look at the moon, drink coffee and dream.

A chair, a fishing rod, a cup of coffee, a small battery-powered radio and the beach came together to become a kind of refuge for me. Yes, there was a lot of waiting and disappointment—most of the time I didn't catch anything—but there was more. Fishing can show you the essence of the conflict in life and the methods of survival and victory. It was a battle between me and things I couldn't see (the fish) and things I couldn't change or control (tides, the heat, rain, the fog, the position of the moon). I discovered through fishing that I could rise to the challenge of that endless battle, renewed each time I cast the hook into the water. Mostly I lost, but each catch was proof that I was capable of challenging the waves.

Holding the fishing rod, feeling the line under the water, being ready for the unexpected, anticipating the fish, not giving up—you develop a new kind of feeling for things that exist even if you can't see them. The same skills l learned from fishing helped me later at the airport, where I also sat on a chair, with a cup of coffee and radio, closing my eyes and anticipating the challenge of the unde-feated system. When I was fishing, I refused to leave until I had a least one catch, my proof of victory, even though I had no way to cook it and always ended up giving it away.

My favourite spot to fish was in a very wealthy area in Abu Dhabi, a very small beach lined with palaces belonging to sheikhs, ambassadors and the high-ranking foreign experts without whom the country can't function. Each palace had a security post at the gate, and the guards would watch me from a distance, sometimes shouting at me to leave or to move my car so it wouldn't disturb the view in case one of the sheikhs decided to look out his window. I don't know why I liked it so much. Perhaps because it was quiet, as most people stayed away, intimidated by the palaces. Or maybe because, as Arabic wisdom says, "the best place for the thief to hide is on the roof of the police station."

One hot summer afternoon, an hour before the sunset, I was there standing next to my fishing rod, wearing a huge hat and long sleeves to protect myself from the sun, sweating and thinking that if I had a place to stay I would rather not fish in this hell. Out of nowhere came a short man in his early sixties, wearing orange pajama bottoms, an orange T-shirt and gold-framed spectacles. He was bald on top with long hair flowing from the sides of his scalp and held one hand over a stomach that strained against the T-shirt. He said, "Hi. What are you doing?"

I looked at this weird man carefully, before deciding how to reply.

Questions with obvious answers I can never take seriously, and I always end up answering with irony or sarcasm, which upsets people most of the time. I have tried to stop this, but I cannot resist watching their reaction, a sparkle of anger in their eyes, and then the moment when they realize, "Yeah! That was a silly question."

"What does it look like I am doing, sir? I am feeding the fish."

Despite his odd appearance, he got my joke and walked towards me. He took the fishing rod and started reeling the line in.

"I can help you with that. What are you feeding them anyway?"

"Shrimp."

"I have never fished from the shore, this is my first time. I saw you from the window, so I thought I should come and join you. Where are you from?"

"Syria. Which window exactly?"

Alarm bells were ringing in my head. This was a neighbourhood of palaces, and here I was talking to someone who lived in one of them. What was I thinking, exposing myself, an illegal man with a fishing rod, in a high-security area?

Moving his head above his shoulder, he pointed with his chin at one of the palaces behind us.

"That window over there, behind you."

"Great," I replied. It was hard for me to hide the resentment I was feeling.

"It's sad what is going on there in Syria. Are you supporting the regime or the opposition?"

That was the usual and expected question, the one everyone asked Syrians after the war started, right after they had expressed their sadness about it. It didn't matter what your answer was; they would follow up with their own political and military analysis without missing their favourite subject for all times and crises, the Sunni and Shia conflict.

I didn't want to talk about it, and I was not about to ask him to introduce himself, which would mean I would have to introduce myself too. That would lead to awkward questions like where did I work. I needed an escape plan, and I found it.

"You say you've never fished off the shore before? How come, since you live ten metres away from it? If I were the one living here, and that is never going to happen, but if I were the one, I would do nothing but fish off the shore."

"I have a yacht."

"Of course you do. What I was thinking! Okay, you are right. I would probably do that."

"I work for the sheik and we go together."

I did not ask which sheik, he did not tell me either. The Emiratis tend not to name them in any case, as the mystery is their way of showing off—they could be working for the president himself, the crown prince, one of his sons, brothers or grandsons. No one knows, and they never mention what kind of work they do. Is he an adviser, driver, cook? No one knows that either.

"It was a pleasure meeting you. Unfortunately, I need to go now."

Two days later, same time of day, same place, I was there and he showed up again.

"Hello. How is the fish feeding going?"

Great. The orange guy again. That's it, I told myself. This is the last time I am going to fish here. "It's going well. Thanks for asking. How is your day going so far?" Those who work for sheiks are busier than they look.

"I was with him last night, and I told him about you."

"Say what? What did you tell him?"

"That a Syrian guy came here to fish and he left with nothing."

I wish you told him that I left with nothing because you showed up, sir. "Oh, yeah, and what did he say?"

"He said, we have our freezers full of fish. Give him some."

"And what did you answer him?"

"I told him it's not a matter of getting food. He is not coming here because he is hungry, it's just a hobby."

"Thank you."

The UAE poses as a modern country, but the relationship between the Royal Family and their people was and still is based on tradition. For his sheik to say what he said was his way of ruling his people. It said, "I am the ruler and this is my land, my money. I own everything and whatever I give you is thanks to me and my generosity." It is the custom for sheiks to host a reception twice a week, where people can come and ask for favours—land to

build a house, money to pay a debt, funds for a son's wedding—
and it's up to the sheik to give or not.

While the orange man was helping me fish for the second time,
he told a story. Perhaps he thought I still had a lot to learn.

"I have a friend from the UK, and she used to live here in
that palace. She went to visit Syria before the war, and when she
came back I asked her about her impressions. 'They live in small
houses,' she said, 'not in a big villa like the ones you have here, but
warm, clean, with some simple and maybe cheap art and imitation
antiques, but they do have libraries. They have no servants, drivers
or gardeners, but they all sit together at dinner time, eat together,
and they will wait if someone is running late. They seem to find
a way to be happy with the little they have. They do care about
education and culture. They have civilization and a long history;
they smile to your face and never want you to leave.'"

He put down the fishing rod, looked at me and drew a long
breath, to show that he was reflecting on what she had said. "She
was trying not to hurt me, but I got it, what she was actually
saying—there is a difference between our peoples, although we
were both Arabs in her eyes. I have visited Syria so many times,
and I love it there. We both share a lot of habits, but I think
money has spoiled us. What do you think?"

During my time among the people of the Arabic Peninsula,
I'd learned a number of things about them. Most of them liked
the money and luxury, their gleaming cities, but somehow they
distrusted modernity as a threat to their Bedouin spirit and the
essence of their faith. Few used their wealth to educate themselves
and to travel, to learn about other civilizations and cultures. Their
money and labour system made them act as if they were superior.
We foreign workers reinforced that; teachers, mostly from Syria
and Egypt, never failed local students, leaking the answers to exam
questions to make sure they always passed, even if they didn't

study. He had been telling the story to himself as much as to me and it felt as if he were describing my family. I understood what he was talking about and what he was expecting. It seemed like he was giving me permission to give him a direct, frank answer.

"When was this, sir?"

"Three years ago."

"And you still remember it! Why?"

"I don't know, but whenever I meet a Syrian, I remember it."

"It's hard to tell. Money can build you towers and highways, and life is damn easier if you have it. A man can run with his bare feet, but it will hurt less if he has a pair of Adidas. Civilization helps you accumulate experience, money can't do that. There is a gap you need to fill, a gap between the camel and the Range Rover."

He shook his head, waited a minute, looked at me and without saying a single word, turned his back and returned to his palace and his sheik, hiding the truth behind the long walls and the tall palm trees, but never from himself.

Did I intend to hurt him that day? I don't know if I was speaking what I believed to be true, or if it was just an angry reaction to what I was going through. It was a meaningless victory, one that made me feel better for a moment, seeing the look in his eyes and the humiliation he was hiding. I wish I could take it back and apologize. Here was a man who understood the problem, was just confirming it to me. I knew that, and still, instead of helping someone who was feeling sad, instead of encouraging him to continue speaking the truth, I beat him down further. That is something I am trying never to do again. I continued to fish at the same place for years, but I never saw him again.

Maybe I was looking back through happy memories to help me through difficult times, or maybe it was me regretting my mistakes. In any case, I thought a lot about my friends, and it made me feel

angry and betrayed. I thought about them while I was staring at the
metal roof of the car I was living in, and while charging my cellphone sitting on the floor in the main entrance of some building.
I thought about them as I watched the sun rise or set while I was
fishing, thinking how it would be nice to have someone with me.
Later I would think about them as I sat on a chair staring at the
runway in Kuala Lumpur Airport, and when I stood in a crowded
prison cell with no space to move. And I think about them now,
here in Canada, as I try to make new friends.

But it was not just the fault of my friends, it was my fault too.
When I came to the UAE, I had a lot of people I thought of as
friends, people from Sweida whom I had not previously met,
acquaintances within our social circle. I was too proud to tell them
about my situation or to accept their charity, so I would usually wait
for them to invite me to visit and play some cards. I was afraid of
their reaction. How would they take it? Are they going to judge me
or help me? If so, how are they going to help? What can they do?
They had space, so I don't think they minded when I sometimes
called them, but it wasn't right to stay and not pay, so I started keeping my distance. I not only ran and hid from my problems, I ran
from the people around me, people who might care about me.

Hunger and the instinct for survival will push you to the edge of
the impossible and irrational; some will blame life and society for
what is happening to them and drift to criminal activities, using
what they are going through as an excuse to justify their crimes. I
myself considered it, but whenever I did, I would call my mother
or father, and their voices over the phone would be enough to force
me back to reality. I could not do that to them, I could not risk
the chance of not seeing them again, so I tried to find any kind of
work, anything to fill my stomach, but with no legal status it was
almost impossible.

Money is the lifeblood, and having it would solve a lot of

problems, and I was in need of it. It was now 2015 and in addition to my illegality problems—no work permit, no passport—a number of police cases had been opened against me for late payment on my credit cards. Every time my phone rang, I jumped and ignored it. The callers were now the police and debt collection agencies. Switching my cellphone to silent only helped me to avoid my problems, not solve them. To this day, I always keep my ringer turned off; old habits born of anxiety and fear don't die easily.

I had a wristwatch, a big modern one with a brown leather strap. It was a knock-off but beautiful, and I had bought it years ago when I was first working in Dubai. It cost me 250 Dirham (about US$70), and I was wearing it when I walked by a Pakistani bakery, a small shop popular in the neighbourhood, with the reputation of making the best handmade bread. The baker was seated above the oven, making the long, dimpled loaves that were cheap and eaten hot and fresh. For just a little more, they would add some extra toppings. It had been two days since I'd eaten or drunk anything other than water and I could not resist the smell. I walked in with no money in my pocket, dirty, sweaty and hungry. I offered to trade my watch for some bread. The young Pakistani guy looked surprised—this was an unusual situation.

"What is wrong?" he asked me. I just smiled and said nothing. He smiled back; of course, he knew the feeling that life was hard and unfair, he was sitting above a hot oven in an overheated country trying to make living. He invited me to sit, gave me some cold water, then a glass of tea. I've never been a tea person, but that extra sweet tea was what I needed. He let me charge my cellphone and he let me rest. Before I left, I gave him my watch and he gave me three loaves of bread with added cheese and olive oil with thyme.

At that time I was sleeping on the staircase of a building I was familiar with, and where I knew the wi-fi password. Few people use the stairs in these large buildings, mostly the elevators, but still I had to be alert to any sound, footsteps or a door opening. I would pretend I was going up or down the stairs, depending on whether the noise was coming from above or below. Most of the time, I hid from people, with that one question in my mind, What should I do next? The end was beginning, the signals were obvious, but I felt there was nothing I could do about it except wait for destiny and the day I would have to turn myself in.

A good day was one when I had one dirham (twenty-five cents) to buy a small cup of coffee from an Indian coffee shop, only Nescafe with some hot water, but enough for me to start my day. It was a luxury I did not always get. I used to sleep in my car in front of the café, waiting for the sun to rise and the place to open at 6:00 a.m. One morning, after I'd bought my Nescafe, I decided to change my parking spot, as I could not risk being seen waiting in one place for too long. The minute I started the engine, a police car pulled up and blocked my way. An officer got out and started walking toward me.

Hundreds of thoughts and voices filled my head during the seconds it took him to reach me and knock on my window. *It's time! It's finally happening! Do I turn myself in? What should I say to him?* I was afraid, but mostly I felt shame. Cursing the unfairness, the bad luck or blaming God for sending a police officer my way at six in the morning was no help. What mattered was how to escape this, to focus on the lies I needed to convince him with. I needed to breathe normally and not show my fear and who I was—a jobless, homeless illegal. I was a man who was free to have a cup of coffee anytime I wanted to. I lowered my window.

"*Al Salam Alaykum*, officer. It's six in the morning! Did you dream about me last night?"

"*Wa Alaykum Al Salam*. Registration and licence please."

"Listen, I don't have them. I just came up for coffee before heading to work. I'm going back to my home to get dressed and I left everything there. I live in that building (I pointed toward the first building I saw). I did not expect to be stopped by the police so early in the morning."

I needed him not to ask me my name, as the moment he did a search he would find the warrants. So I spoke continuously, stopping only when I needed to breathe.

"Come on—I am just having my first cup of coffee! Not a good way to start the day by having a fine. Give me a break, please!" While I was saying this, I got out of the car, holding my cup of coffee up to his face, making sure that I had the keys and cigarettes in my pocket.

"I will tell you what. If you insist, I can go to my house and bring you what you ask for. I live just over there. It will take me a minute."

He looked at me. "Go. Bring them here. I will wait."

"Thank you, officer. Thank you so much."

I walked away and before I went too far, I took the car keys from my pocket and pressed the remote lock button. Holding my cup of coffee and not looking behind me, I entered a building and didn't go back. An hour later I called a former colleague from the oil company and asked him to meet me and move the car. I didn't tell him why. I was afraid the police officer might still be waiting.

While I was hiding in the backyard of the building, waiting for my friend to come and move the car, I drank my coffee and smoked a cigarette with a big smile on my face. I felt ridiculously pleased with my victory. I had just defeated the system for the first time. The rebel in me was waking up.

There was another Hassan, the man I thought I should have been—successful, well dressed and well groomed—the one who would have made different choices. He would come to me in my imagination, and whisper in my ear, "Turn yourself in. Give up. At least you will have a bed and food." I'd shake my head and say, "Timing, it's all about timing. I can feel it and it's not the right time yet." Other Hassan would laugh mockingly, shake his head and disappear.

"I told you so," he said to me once. I'd run into a building still under construction—rebar steel bars, cement mixers, heavy equipment—taking refuge after ending a call with my family. They'd just told me my father had cancer and I wanted a place to cry alone. It was one of the weakest, most defeated moments of my life. "You were right," I said to Other Hassan. "If I'd turned myself in when you told me to, I would be home with him now."

I leaned my forehead against one of the steel bars and banged my head against it again and again. "I am sorry. I am sorry. I love you so much."

My hope that something would miraculously change ended in November 2016, when a plainclothes police officer, dressed like a Pakistani guy, knocked on my car window at 1:00 a.m. I held out my hands with no resistance and gave him my full name. He escorted me to his car, one hand pushing my head down, the other holding my handcuffed hands behind my back.

In the back seat of the police car that night, Other Hassan whispered to me, "Man, you are pathetic and powerless. You are done." But I felt strangely relieved. It was like giving myself to a wave after the years of hiding and suffering. I was no longer in charge of myself and, while I was still afraid, it was a different kind of fear. When you know a storm is coming, you're afraid of what might happen, but when you're in the middle of it, sometimes the only way to save yourself is to run into it.

Chapter Five

River of Madness

AT THE POLICE station, the interrogations began. They asked for my cellphone password and then searched through my text messages and WhatsApp conversations. I was confused but learned later there had been a theft in the area that same night and I was a suspect. Two hours later, after they'd checked my shoeprints, they decided I was innocent of that crime and sent me to a holding cell.

I am better than this. I am not a bad guy. I don't deserve to be here. That is what I told myself as I found myself in jail for the first time in my life. Yet there I was, in my new reality, and I needed to deal with it. It was 4:00 a.m. when I lay down on a bunk and closed my eyes, forcing myself not to think about the shame.

In the morning, they transferred me to the central police station and, on the journey, I had a chance to call my family. It was a short call, one I didn't want to make but had to. "I am on my way to the Central Jail," I told Solaf. "I will call you when I can. I am sorry for everything." She was supportive; she knew her brother wasn't a criminal, and this was just a matter of my illegal status and money. All part of the new Syrian tragedy. Next I called the Yemeni guy and asked him to go get the car. He left the office shortly afterward and his replacement threw all my stuff away.

It was dark inside the police car, with black metal webbing running down to my knees. I cursed myself and the war, everyone and everything that had put me in this situation: dictatorship, the army, politics, money, passports, laws. I was no longer the young guy who wanted to travel the world and meet people. I could no longer pretend I was the professional with a nice suit meeting customers, with big dreams and a bright future. I was a criminal in handcuffs, waiting to learn his charges.

I knew what they were going to be: overstaying my visa, money owed. When they read them out to me at the central police station, I kept quiet. There was no point in arguing about the contradictions of the law and its flaws. Save it for the court, when you meet the judge, I told myself. The jails in the UAE were overcrowded with debtors, as it is a criminal offence to fail to make your credit card payments. In the days that followed, as I waited in my cell, I imagined myself standing in front of the judge and prepared my defence. It needed to be brief but meaningful; the judge would have a lot of other cases and I didn't want to bore him or make him feel that I was wasting his time. A minute would be enough to make my point, unemotionally, just the facts. I was going to address the court with respect, look the judge in the eye, and speak with no fear.

"Your Honour, the law says I am not allowed to work unless I have a work permit, but I can't have a work permit if I have a warrant for late payments. How can you expect me to pay my debt if I cannot work? When I was employed, for years I had no problem with my payments, and I have the records to prove this. It is a contradiction, Your Honour: no work without a permit, no permit without payment, no payment without money, no money without work. I am one of those people, Your Honour, who walks in a circle, always returning to the starting point and never able to stop walking."

For the next two months, they shuffled me back and forth

between Emirati states to process the financial cases against me. I never saw a judge, but would be woken in the middle of the night for another transfer to another police station. During the many long midnight journeys, and with every wake-up call, I would think, This is the worst. Then, Wait. The worst is yet to come. I could not have imagined what the worst would be.

While in jail in the UAE, the worst that I could imagine was being sent back to Syria. The fear of being deported was what kept me awake at night; that, and the thought of what might happen the moment I reached Damascus Airport. Instead of confronting my problems and the fear I felt, I'd made excuses to run from them. Now, during each night in different jail cells, I was forced to learn, to gain the self-knowledge, the experience and the strength I would need to face what was to come.

The worst was yet to come, I had said to myself over and over. And then it came. It was New Year's Eve, 2016, and I was in a police station in Sharjah. It was, surprisingly, almost empty, unlike the others I'd been spending time in. I had been there for about a week, waiting for my transfer to Abu Dhabi and what I assumed was going to be the immigration jail. Solaf had used the insurance money from her late husband, which was in a bank in Kuwait, to clear my credit card debts.

Knowing what my next destination was, I didn't mind this police station—it was almost a place for rest and recreation, compared to the others. There were two rooms for six inmates, each with a toilet and hot water taps. There was no bed or furniture, just three thin blankets—one for a mattress, one for a pillow and the other to sleep under. Inmates were allowed to make one phone call each day, after the 5:00 p.m. last meal, on the telephone in the metre-wide passage between the two cells. And there was also a bathroom for the block.

Like every police station, there was the good cop and the bad cop. Here, the good cop was Muhammad, who would keep the cell doors open for us a bit longer than most, and would let the canteen worker bring us some coffee and biscuits. There were two kinds of biscuits, salty and sweet; I always went for the salty and two cups of coffee. You pay attention to the police in your jail, learn their routines and shifts, so you know when good-cop is due to start work, as that means coffee, biscuits and other good things are on their way. That New Year's Eve, we were waiting for Muhammad to start his shift.

One of my five cellmates was from South Africa. He'd been there when I arrived and had a sister who was a flight attendant for Emirates Airlines. She used to visit him almost daily and, like prisoners the world over, he and I would spend our day coming up with plans of how she could smuggle things in for us. We had a lighter, but needed cigarettes to go with our occasional cup of coffee. Our plan was simple: we'd wait for Muhammad, I would distract him and my cellmate's sister would pass the contraband cigarettes through the window in the cell door. The cell doors were always shut when visitors came, no direct personal contact allowed.

When we came up with our plan, I said to him, "If they catch us, we might get into more trouble."

"What's the worst that could happen?" he said, "Are they going to throw us in jail?"

We both laughed, and that was enough to know that we were ready.

The first attempt, the day before New Year's Eve, was a partial success (Muhammad distracted), but the package of cigarettes the sister brought was too big to pass through the window. We were disappointed but determined to try again the next day, New Year's Eve. "Tell your sister to bring slimline cigarettes next time!"

And so she did. Unfortunately, the next day turned out to be bad-cop's shift, but I didn't let that stop me. The sister arrived and I shouted, "Sir, sir!" over and over. "Sir, sir, sir, hurry up!"

"What the hell do you want? Why are you shouting?"

"I just saw a mouse enter your office, a big one. I am telling you, it's almost the size of a cat, it's there in your office and it may eat all your food."

"Are you sure?"

"One hundred percent. I am telling you, it's huge."

"Help me catch it."

And that was it, simple and quick. While bad-cop and I were searching his office for the cat-size mouse, the sister passed ten loose cigarettes through the opening. In the end, bad-cop lost patience with me and shouted, "There is nothing here. Go back to your cell NOW!"

"That damn mouse. It must have run away, sir."

In the bathroom later, my friend and I sat on the floor and smoked a whole cigarette each, trying to enjoy it to the fullest. For both of us, it felt like smoking a victory cigar.

Smoking that cigarette helped set me up for that evening's telephone call. My father's health had been deteriorating since he had started chemotherapy, but I naively thought it might just be complications from the treatment and that he would get better soon. I wanted to speak to him, hear that he was improving. My family had not told me how bad it really was.

I made the call, but all I heard was crying, then silence as the phone was passed to someone else, then more crying. No one was able to speak. The house was full of weeping people, and incomprehensible voices came down the line to me standing in that narrow passageway in a Sharjah police station. It seemed like I could hear the tears falling.

It was Ammar who finally managed to speak without tears as he pulled himself together, the man of the moment. Summoning all possible force, knowing where I was and what I was facing, he managed three short sentences, "Our father is no longer with us. Be strong, brother. We love you."

I collapsed, still holding the receiver in my hand. My eyes closed, my mind filled with the face of the man I had loved. I knew I would never hear his voice again and that I had let him down in his final days. He died feeling anxiety and fear for me, instead of me being at his side, holding his hand, wiping his forehead to place a kiss upon it. If I were to look into his eyes at that moment, I would not feel his pride, but my shame.

I begged for another call that night, but they would not allow it. I desperately needed to speak to my mother, Solaf and Ammar. I wanted to hear their voices, to comfort them as the elder son should do. Five times that night I left the cell for the bathroom, so I could cry without anyone seeing me. I heard the sound of fireworks outside, and for the first time was filled with regret that I had not resisted that policeman who had arrested me. If I were outside, I could call them. For the rest of the night, I lay on my side in the cell, looking up at the small window in the wall, waiting for the sun to rise so I could call my family. For the first time I heard the broken voice of my soul and knew that I would never recover from this, ever. I met my new soulmate, sadness, and knew that it would never leave me, even as I survived and would one day choose to smile again.

Ever since that New Year's Eve in 2016, whenever I am working on something, I look up to the left and see my father's face. He tells me if I am doing the right thing or not, and I smile for him and he smiles for me in return.

A year after I arrived in Canada, I was invited to speak to a group of students at the University of British Columbia. Some were interested in what I was saying and others were just waiting for the time to pass so they could get on with what they really wanted to do. I understand that—I remember being like that when I was a student—and I was pleased when I managed to get more of them on board, and they began to ask questions. One student, however, had seemed interested the minute I walked in. She'd paid attention when the professor introduced me the day before. She was young and beautiful and her glasses gave her an intelligent look that spoke of academic excellence. When her turn came, she asked, "Do you feel homesick?" She explained that her mother was an immigrant, but that this was not a question she could ever ask her. The girl sounded worried, and I wished I had an answer that would comfort her.

I remembered that long night at Sharjah police station, and that made me think of the times I would sit with my father and family in the shade of an olive tree at our farm. "There is not a single day your mother doesn't remember her home country," I answered. "It's our destiny to live between two worlds, and no matter where we are, we will miss one of them. It is the small things in our daily life that keep reminding us. For me, it's olives, bread, coffee, rain, snow and music. But your mother—she looks at you every day with pride, you are her happiness and good fortune, and wherever you are will be home to her."

The answer was for me as well, and I looked up to the left to see if my father agreed with me. If I could feel his presence, Canada would now be his home too.

The first five days of 2017, I spoke to no one, except for one call with my mother. I lay on my blanket and stared at the ceiling, two songs going through my head, both my father's favourites: "Hawa Al Wedyan" ("Valley Air") and "Far Away" by Demis Roussos. On the sixth day, they transferred me back to Abu Dhabi. I assumed my next destination was to be the immigration detention centre so they could deport me.

"Kontar! Kontar, Hassan." A police officer holding some documents was shouting my name.

"Yes!"

"Prepare yourself."

"For what exactly?"

"You are going to Central Jail."

"Central Jail! For what? Sir, you are mistaken. I should be sent to immigration."

"No, you are going to the central jail for a crime you committed."

"Don't I need to see the judge or to be sent to a court before you send me to the central jail?"

"There is a court sentence issued against you in advance. You don't need to see the judge. You can appeal after fifteen days while you are there serving your sentence."

Terrified, I tried to see what was written on the paperwork he was holding.

"Crime? Appeal? What are you talking about?"

In the year 2011, you left a cafeteria in Abu Dhabi without paying for your sandwich. Therefore the court has sentenced you to a month in Central Jail."

"Are you serious? Is this a new kind of torture or what? It's 2017 now. I would never do such a thing. And in 2011 I was living in Dubai, not Abu Dhabi. I wouldn't travel a hundred and seventy kilometres to eat in a cafeteria and not pay. Give me the name of the restaurant!"

"I don't have it."

"Are you serious? Give me their phone number then. Someone can go and pay it and they can withdraw the case."

"I don't have it."

"Are you serious? Give me the address, the case number, the bill number, anything!"

"I don't have that either. This was before we started using computers to archive all cases."

My hands pressed to my temples, I paced back and forth.

"You must be kidding me! Are you serious? You want me to wait fifteen days to appeal when my sentence is only a month! If you have no information, how do you know it was me?"

"I have your name written here."

"Did they write what I ate? It must have been a hell of a sandwich."

They handcuffed my hands behind my back and sent me to spend yet another month in jail—no trial, no judge—for a sandwich I did not eat six years ago.

At the Central Jail in Abu Dhabi, they took my fingerprints and another prisoner shaved my head. This was not a place like the other jails, this was the one where the *real* criminals were. Two months before, I had never met an addict, but after my tour of UAE jails, I'd learned about different drugs, how to use them and what the penalty was for possession of each type. What was I going to learn in this place? I knew I needed to look strong and not in mourning, and I should definitely not talk about politics or religion. *Keep a low profile, ride out the sentence, get out of here.* That was the plan, but I am me and I don't know how to keep my mouth shut when I should.

The dirty dark blue uniform they gave me was three times my size. I was placed in Block 8, classified for the minimally dangerous, mainly people in for financial crimes. The block was a quadrangle, with a central, open courtyard. Each cell held six people, and the cell doors that opened onto the walkway were never closed. It was like being imprisoned inside a high balcony. In one corner of the walkway there was a small television. There was an almost casual air about the block, with no patrolling officers, perhaps because those police stations were temporary and this was home for the prisoners. I was a guy who had spent the last two months coming up with plans for how to smuggle in cigarettes or get an extra cup of coffee. Here, we could buy most things from the canteen: coffee, chocolate, hygiene products and Indomie instant noodles.

Hospitality and generosity are important characteristics for Arab people, and the prisoners here had not forgotten the customs. The moment the supervisor escorted me to my cell, the residents welcomed me, gave me clothes and cigarettes, pointed out where they kept the coffee and showed me how to get hot water. Five of them were Jordanian and all were "seniors," having served between two and seven years already.

It was a challenge to act tough and not to show any kind of weakness in front of these men who had spent years behind bars for real crimes while I was there for not paying for a sandwich. When they asked me what I was in for, I dodged the question, but eventually they found my jail card and made fun of me for the rest of my sentence.

The inmates had nothing to do all day but smoke, drink coffee and play cards. They had a league chart for cards: who was playing with whom, how many times you'd won or lost. We Arabs love to play cards, not for money—gambling is shameful—but for the fun and competition. I hadn't played cards regularly for years, not since leaving Syria, but when I was younger I won a lot and had a reputation as a good player.

For the first few days, I kept my distance, observing, not engaging much, and not giving any sign that I knew how to play. I did ask about a prison library, or how to get a book. On my way to Block 8, I'd seen photos in the hallway of the Crown Prince of Abu Dhabi smiling at groups of inmates reading in a library and others being trained in a workshop.

"There is a library, but you need to register. And you can't bring any books out. Books are not allowed in the cells," was what they told me. I didn't bring up the subject of the photos, because the block next to ours was Block 9, for political prisoners, and I had no desire to move there.

It took four days for my library approval to come through. While I was waiting, I used to sit outside the cell with my coffee, a cigarette and a small radio one of my cellmates had loaned me, trying to connect with the outside world and follow the news coming from Syria. It was hard to nap in my cell because the card players would shout at each other for playing badly.

One day, I asked one them, "How long have you been here?"

"Two and a half years."

"What did you do?"

"Fraud."

"Is this your first time?"

"No, the third."

"How often do you play cards?"

"Every day."

"You practise every day for the last two and a half years and still don't know how to play? Weird. But I think your card-playing skills are the same as your money skills. You lose with both!"

The players laughed and asked me: "What should he do instead?"

"In fraud or cards?"

"Cards."

"He should have played this card instead of that one," I said, as I took his cards and went over what had been played.

One man, who was known as the boss of the cell, having lived there for seven years, smiled and asked, "What about fraud?"

"He is not good at that either, otherwise he would not be here for the third time already. Clearly, he is not learning anything from his mistakes, and the minute he is out he will do it again and come back here."

"Let us hope for your sake that you know how to play the same way you talk. You are going to play next and I will be your partner."

Cell Boss had challenged me. He didn't want to lose to me, and by making me his partner, if we lost, he would be able to blame me. For me, I saw that winning at cards would be my way into the group. I would not be an outsider anymore. Perhaps I might start to feel normal again if they included me; at least it would help me pass the time and would also give me some protection if I needed it. I thought of the play, *The River of Madness*, by the Egyptian Tawfiq Al-Hakim, that discussed the value of the mind in the midst of a crazed kingdom. So I decided to be as crazy as they were in order to survive.

Cell Boss and I won, and from then on, I became popular. They'd make me coffee and share their creative solutions for getting by: making weightlifting equipment from plastic Pepsi bottles attached to a stick and filled with water, using empty cigarette cartons as storage drawers, using a small battery to light a cigarette. They also taught me how to use cigarettes as currency. This knowledge (along with how to prepare noodles in a variety of different ways) would all be invaluable when I was trapped at the airport.

Each day, I would spend three hours in the library, the maximum time allowed. The books weren't organized or catalogued, and there was no point in asking the guard on duty in charge, because he could barely write his own name, and knew nothing about the books on the shelves he was guarding. I discovered a collection of great Arabic novels, including *Cities of Salt*, by Abdul Rahman Munif, in which he wrote about how the Gulf cities had been born. For many days, I waited impatiently for my three hours so I could continue reading it—it spoke to me of my own experience of the UAE. Later, I read on Google that the author had explained the title of his book with this: "Oil is our one and only chance to build a future. It means cities that offer no sustainable existence. When the waters come in, the first waves will dissolve the salt and reduce these great glass cities to dust. In antiquity, as you know, many cities simply disappeared. It is possible to foresee the downfall of cities that are inhuman. With no means of livelihood, they won't survive."

For some, prison is a place they become attached to. The daily routine is a relief, they have their own space and respect among their fellow inmates, they have a value in jail that they don't have outside, and they can be themselves. But for me it was dangerous—I was no longer attached to the outside world and, more importantly, I felt as if my dreams were dead. As an adult, we have dreams that are aims and goals. If one of those dreams is not meant to be, we consign it to our past and focus on the others. Our dreams are related to the reality of who we are. To dream of being an astronaut while serving a ten-year prison sentence is not a dream, it is a fantasy. To dream of the day they release you, to live in peace and start again, this is a realistic and legitimate dream. It's also a necessary one, and if you lose that while inside prison walls, your soul will die.

This came to me vividly on the first Monday of my sentence in Block 8. The lights were off, cards were over and most people went to their cells and, as on other nights, a few inmates would watch the TV in the corner of the walkway. This Monday night was different. Every cell including mine was empty. Where was everyone?

Someone passed my open cell door.

"What in God's name is going on?" I asked him. "Have the guards opened the gates? Where is everyone?"

"Watching TV," he said, with a smile that said, "What kind of silly joke is this?"

"Has something serious happened? Are they watching the news?"

"No, man, it's Monday night."

"So?"

"It's the night when they show Bollywood movies. Every Monday and Thursday night."

"Last night they showed a Hollywood movie and I did not see you watching that."

"Yes, but this is Bollywood. Bollywood!"

"Interesting," I said to myself as he walked away to sit in the place designated for him according to his seniority.

I made a cup of coffee, lit up a cigarette and went to stand behind the audience focused on the small TV screen. With their unblinking eyes and slack jaws, they were clearly in another world.

Why Bollywood? It didn't take me long to understand.

Everything is there in one movie: superheroes, music, dancing, beautiful actresses, money, cars, fights, drama, love, laughter. And, most important of all, the happy ending. The ending is always happy in Bollywood movies, and that was exactly what these men wanted every Monday and Thursday night, everything they were missing. Their dreams were no longer related to who they were and what they might do, those were fantasies. They were disconnected from their lives and their only way to carry on was to imagine themselves as the hero in a Bollywood movie, living that unreal life so that by the time they went to bed, they could close their eyes and imagine themselves living the movie they had just watched. They didn't want to watch films where the heroes were moral human beings, who sacrificed themselves for principles. Heroes like that represented all they were not and reminded them of the immoral acts they'd committed for which they were being punished. For them, self-sacrifice was the equivalent of wasting life. They wanted romantic dreams of saving their beloved from evil villains. How do I know that? Because for one month I was one of them. They opened their closed circle, trusted me and let me in.

Films were a big part of my life during the years of running and hiding away. Movies based on real stories, politics and history, ones that looked at big issues and morality, were and still are my favourites. During the 2016 US presidential campaign, I remember President Obama comparing Donald Trump to a character in *The Hunger Games*. I was homeless at the time, overwhelmed with problems, but politics still absorbed me and I was following the election on my cellphone, sitting in the driver's seat of the car I called home. I wondered how Trump might affect the war in Syria if he won.

President Obama's comment made me want to see the movie—how could such a movie be involved in the election? Would it help me understand more about Mr. Trump's personality? One evening, when I was visiting friends for a day or two, they turned on the television and there it was, *The Hunger Games: Mockingjay, Part 1.*

"You guys might want to watch this," I said.

"What is it?"

"It's a movie used by President Obama to make fun of Mr. Trump." I knew this would not be enough to get their attention, so I added: "The main character is played by a very beautiful actress."

"Oh. Okay then. What is it about?"

"In my opinion, if you forget about the idea of the games and killing, it's about the Syrian war. Watching it will give you a better understanding of what is happening or, at least, it will make you think in a different way. President Obama was wrong to use it to mock Trump."

"Huh! What in God's name are you talking about?"

"Just watch it, and I will explain."

We binge-watched the whole series, not sleeping but discussing and debating over coffee, tea and chips until 6:00 a.m. We talked about what the film was about and its connection to events in Syria. We talked about dictatorships, and how with our revolution against it and our pursuit of change, we had accidentally replaced it with an even harsher regime. We hadn't noticed it, because all we were concerned with was getting rid of the current government, the evil one we knew, not seeing the evil one we didn't know about yet. We talked about the media and its coverage of the war, about its influence and how it shaped public opinion. We talked about the devastation caused while trying to build a better society and the victims of dictatorships—how everyone could be used as a disposable tool to gain or hold power. Most importantly, we talked about heroes and how they are made, how they can inspire others without having the ambition to do so. Do they remain revolutionaries, even when the war is over? I saw the movie three times.

Shortly after I was arrested, as I was being transferred to a new police station, they walked me past a wall-mounted TV in the prison guard's room. That was the moment I learned that Donald Trump had been elected president. Months earlier, an American teacher in Abu Dhabi had told me that people in the USA were sick of the traditional political families and how they are providing nothing but unfulfilled promises. I had hoped that this was only her opinion and not the prevailing mood across the ocean. Even the guards and officers were upset; they did not want him in the Gulf and they knew from the first minute that he would be after their money.

Time is counted differently in prison. In the outside world, one month is thirty-one days, but at the Central Jail, they ignore Saturdays and Sundays, and add those twelve days to the total, making thirty-five days. From Day 23, I asked when I would be released; the answer was always, "We are reviewing your file."

I would respond with a smile, "No rush, it's just [one, five, eleven] days past the due date."

My cellmates hugged me and walked me to the block's main door when it was finally my time to go. We exchanged numbers, in case any of them were set free too; some asked me to call their family, to pass messages on. My thoughts were heavy as I left, preparing myself for the final stage of my time in the UAE. What was going to happen next? As they marched me to the police van, I took a final look at what had been my home for thirty-five days. There are some good people inside, I told myself. Criminals, yes. They did something illegal, yes. Greedy and looking for easy money, yes. Am I going to miss them? Yes, absolutely. Am I going to remember them for the rest of my life, wondering about their news and how they are doing, with the hope that they will learn their lesson and never go back to Central Jail Block 8 again? Yes.

The immigration jail is next to Central Jail, and my cellmates had said they would probably walk me over. Instead, I was put into a police van and driven for about forty minutes before we stopped.

What none of us knew was that the old immigration jail had been closed down as unsuitable for human (even prisoner) habitation. A new one was under construction, not completely finished, and the sheikh ordered the authorities to open it, even if it wasn't ready yet. That was my destination.

It was a Sunday morning, around 11:00 a.m. and I was part of the second batch of prisoners to be sent to the new installation. The first group had arrived the Thursday before. My accumulated experience of Emirati police stations made me realize there was something not right with this place. Computers weren't plugged in, desks and chairs were still covered in plastic wrapping. The guards transporting us clearly didn't know what to do. "We can organize it later," one of the officers said, and so they left us, and our files, and just locked us inside.

There was a TV crew there, covering an inspection visit by the General Director of Police. I looked at the man, with all the officers around him, the centre of everything and the only still, constant figure, as others moved around as if trying to catch up and please him. Power and authority were manifested in front of me—handcuffed, unable to have a drink of water or stand or sit without permission—in their clearest form. This man with his gun at his waist, surrounded by companions, was two metres away from me. He could solve my legal status with just one word, I thought. That's how things run in this part of the world.

I was tempted. A voice in my head said, It's now or never. Do something, it's your chance. Part of me wanted to call out to him, draw his attention to me, so I could explain my situation—maybe he would help me. But something held me back; I was afraid of humiliating myself. I'm done with this country, I told myself. I have seen enough and witnessed enough. I just want to leave and have a new start, a fresh one, with a clean record. So I said nothing to the man with the gun. Later, I sat on the top bunk of a metal bed. In prison, everyone wants the bottom bunk except me. Although the block was almost empty, I chose the top bunk, which was a little closer to the small window and the sky. As I tried to look out that window at the top of the wall to see the world outside, I regretted my decision not to speak to the director, to take my chance.

The new prison was a prefabricated building outside the city in the middle of nowhere, its yellow colour like the desert sand. The highway to a military base and Dubai was not far away. Metal and cement overlapped in five large blocks that were linked by arcades. A large square inside the walls was used as a parking area for the guards and officers. I saw the square twice, the day they jailed me and the day they set me free, twenty-two days later. On one side of the square were trailers, hastily repurposed as administrative offices when the sheikh had ordered the prison be opened.

Each block had five rows of bunk beds, enough for one hundred and fifty prisoners. There were six separate, doorless rooms which were the bathrooms with showers. As it was newly opened, these were still clean. There were a few Arabs in each block, but I was the only Syrian in mine; the rest were from Egypt, Jordan and Palestine, five or six of us altogether. The other prisoners were from Asian countries: Pakistan, India, Sri Lanka and Bangladesh. None were from Europe or North America.

Signs on the wall indicated where TVs and telephones were to be affixed, but none had been installed. It was like torture to see those signs twenty-four hours a day, but not those little material luxuries. There was no canteen, no library. Three times a day they escorted us to the kitchen, ten metres away, and that was our recreation. On the second day, I looked around and thought, Nothing in life is guaranteed, not even jails. God, I am going to miss Block 8. I should have had one more cup of coffee and one more cigarette before I left Central Jail. I should have listened to one more song on the small radio or read one more chapter from any book.

No one, including the officers, had any idea what was going on. They seemed as lost as we were. The real suffering was on weekends because there was no hope of anything happening or any progress. Each Thursday evening, I prayed, Please let this be the last weekend for me here. I would walk around inside the block until I couldn't feel my feet anymore, then I would climb into my bunk, close my eyes and create my own TV in my head, remembering scenes from favourite movies. Sometimes I sang, but I have a terrible voice (so does Ammar, but not Solaf and my mother, who have beautiful singing voices). I'd laugh at myself and whisper, "Music is not an entertainment. It's a human need, and as long as I need it I will keep singing." I didn't engage with any of the other detainees.

Now that I was at the immigration detention centre, I knew my time was running out. Without a passport, I was going to be sent back to Syria, and the military would be waiting for me at Damascus Airport. But I had not spent six years of my life hiding, running from my destiny, far from my family at the time they needed me the most, just to join the army in the end, even if that meant prison or being sent to the frontline of the war. I had done what I did because of fundamental principles and I needed to keep them, no matter what the cost.

While they were transferring me from Central Jail to the new detention centre, the guards gave me my possessions to hold for the journey. At the other end, I knew that I would have to hand them back. This was a precious opportunity. I turned my cellphone on, with one eye on the escort guards, and checked the battery power: five, six percent left. As quickly as I could, I texted Jehad. "I am on my way to the immigration detention centre. It's a new prison, have no idea where it's located. I need my passport renewed. Do something. Bye." I had always thought that somehow I would find a way to solve my own problems and still be the educated, cultured, smart guy I wanted my friends to see. But now I knew I had no other options and nothing to lose. I didn't know if he received my message or not, if he was going to be able to do anything or not. Just thinking about it on that metal bunk bed or while I walked endlessly was driving me crazy. Anticipation, fear, hope, dread—there was a weight on my chest that made breathing difficult.

Like many people, I sought comfort with the help of faith and prayers. I am Druze, but I have never been very religious, maybe because of the way I was raised. It is a closed religion, surrounded by secrecy and mystery, even for those of us within it. We agree with Islam on the prophets and the Quran, but we differ on other things. We don't pray five times a day, perform Hajj to Mecca or fast during the month of Ramadan, and we don't practise polygamy. Druze is a mixture of religions and philosophies, including Greek. We give the mind a special, sacred place, and we have been called "the people of wisdom." We believe if you want to know about the religion, then you need to abandon your life and dedicate yourself to it. This ambiguity gives others the opportunity to accuse us of not being part of Islam. Fear of being persecuted or judged makes us hesitate before we disclose that we are Druze in Arab countries where we don't exist.

Five months after I arrived in Canada, a fundraising group invited me to speak at their event to sponsor LGBT refugees from Syria and Iraq. It was being held at St. Andrew's Wesley United Church in Vancouver, a historical building whose beauty was not affected by the maintenance work that was going on at the time. We were all there to celebrate a noble cause, in the name of God, love and human rights, coming together to help refugees who were facing discrimination and danger because of their sexual orientation. Walking into the building, I was moved that such an event was taking place in a church. It made me remember the two churches in Sweida. One shared a wall with my high school, and whenever we decided to skip class, we would climb it and jump into the churchyard. We'd land next to the white statue of the Virgin Mary, standing in the corner with her right hand raised as if she were saying hello. "Hey, Mary, please don't tell on us," we'd joke. That was the Eastern Orthodox church; the other one was for Catholics.

During my talk, I introduced Syria and Syrian history and, since it was in a church, I mentioned the town of Maaloula, explaining that it is the only place on Earth where ancient Aramaic, the mother tongue of Jesus, is still spoken. When I'd finished my speech and answered some questions, we got to the part when people normally clap and I go back to my seat. The priest stood up and politely asked me, "Do you believe in God? What faith do you follow?" His question got everyone's attention, and they seemed to be wondering if it was right to ask such a question.

I smiled and cracked a joke, "It's starting to get hot in here," and pretended to wipe sweat from my forehead. I wanted to cool the tension in the room. Then I answered. "Father, since the first dawn, there was God, and there was killing in His name. If he approved such behaviours, then call me an atheist. If He does not approve it—and I believe He does not—then we need to understand that religion, any religion, is nothing but a path toward the goal. Knowing God is the goal, and once we agree on that, we will know that there is nothing wrong with any religion, but only with some of the followers who are acting on its behalf. God is absolute perfection, nothing less and nothing more."

The real test of faith and your belief system, whatever it may be, is when life pushes you beyond your limit; if you can look at yourself, hold your ground and your principles, you can get through all the pain. We are programmed to think of "religion" when we say "faith" or "belief system," but I believe that faith is also truth, justice, freedom and human rights; it's your obligation and duty as a human being. It's not about if you believe that God exists or not, if you pray or not, it's about if you respect those who do, no matter how they do it.

In that new detention prison, I prayed to God directly, but with no formality and rules; I'd just talk to him while I was walking my legs numb, opening my heart and praying for whatever superpower he had to help me, give me a break, and look after my family.

My daily monologue with God or whoever is up there paid off. Somehow, Jehad found a way to get me a new passport, not just the old one renewed, but a brand new one, valid for two years. I still don't know how he did it—pulling strings, calling in favours, paying money. I didn't ask and he didn't want me to.

I held it in my hands, opened it and saw, for the first time in almost six years, I had a valid passport.

"Where did you get the photo from?" was the only question I asked him.

"Ammar sent it to me from Syria."

This precious visit from Jehad was on Day 15 of my time at the immigration detention centre. I could feel hope flowing into my body, running through my blood and giving me the energy to pace around the block despite the pain in my legs. That evening, I sat next to a group of guys who were playing a game they'd marked on the floor using orange peel. "Tonight I will play with you guys. Will you teach me how?"

Now, with a passport, I could request deportation to Malaysia, the logical choice. The flight to Kuala Lumpur was a direct one, with no transfers, meaning no transit visas were required. It was also one of the few countries that did not require Syrians to obtain a visa in advance, before travelling. We could enter with an arrival visa that permitted us to stay for three months. So Syrians being deported from the UAE usually went to Malaysia; it was the easiest option and the one with the least risk.

I had been unable to speak to my family, as no calls were allowed at the detention centre. Not knowing what they were going through made me desperately worried for them. I wanted to explain what

I needed to some senior officers, but the guards blocked me. Sometimes they lied to me, sometimes they ignored me, but they wouldn't let me speak to anyone higher up. They were employed by a private security company, one I knew was owned by one of the sheiks, and weren't locals. They were Moroccans, Jordanians, Somalis, Sudanese and Nepalese, all doing their job of pleasing their master. I would stand next to the shiny new white bars of the block's door and try to communicate with them.

"You know, this is just a job for you. But it's not who you are. This is not your country and you are not a government employee. The minute they are done with you, they will terminate your contract and you may end up on my side of the door. Remember that the next time you are acting tough. You are not even allowed to carry a gun, and despite your military uniform, you are just the stick they hit us with, and the minute you are broken, they will replace you. If you somehow think that you are heroes who are saving the city from criminals like me, you need to wake up. This place is for illegals and refugees, not serial killers. One day you might be one of us."

On Day 19, I finally managed to see a senior officer, who promised to help me to start working on getting a ticket to Malaysia. He even wished me luck when he said goodbye. I could not sleep after that night and stood waiting by the barred door, hoping to hear my name called. The door to the block was designed to be opened remotely, but for some reason the guards still used a key. Each time I heard the keys in the lock, my heart leapt—were they coming for me, was I going to be free at last? Each time I was disappointed.

Three days later, I finally heard my name called. It was just after 5:00 p.m., not the usual time they called the names of those who had a flight out of the UAE that day. I walked the long, dark corridor with the guard without asking him who wanted me or what was going on. I found myself facing the same senior officer I'd met earlier.

"Hassan, you are not allowed to travel."

"What! Why?" I began to shake as I never had before. This had to be some kind of mistake.

"You have a travel ban, so you can't fly. You need to remove it."

"What travel ban? Who banned me? How do I remove it?"

"In 2011, you did not pay for a sandwich, and although you served your sentence, the travel ban was not removed. That has to be done separately."

"You must be kidding! How could a sandwich cause me all of this trouble? I spent thirty-five days in jail for it, and now twenty-two days here. What is the restaurant's name, for the love of God?"

"Please sit," the officer said. He seemed to feel my pain.

"I just don't get it! The things that keep happening to me, they make no sense. It's unbelievable. Just tell me, please, what is going on and what is next? What is it you want me to do? What is it this country wants from me? I am not allowed to have a work visa, and now I am not allowed to leave!"

"I thought this was good news for you," the man said.

"How come?"

"Other prisoners here will write a fake cheque to someone on the outside, just so they can sue them and receive a travel ban. That way they are released from here and can stay in the country."

"Well, that is just wrong! I want to be legal, I want to have a work visa. I don't want to work off-grid. What those guys are doing is releasing themselves from a small prison to a bigger one, with no hope of ever leaving this country. What am I supposed to do two years from now when my passport expires? When will I ever be able to see my family again?"

"Here is what I can do. I am going to release you today. I just need you to call a friend to come and guarantee you with his passport."

"Why did you keep me for twenty-two days then, when you knew there was a travel ban against me?"

"We only discovered it this morning, while we were making the final check before booking you a flight."

"Nice! I have no one to guarantee me but myself. I don't know where to go if you release me now—it's almost 6:00 p.m."

He was kind and polite and appeared to feel sorry for me. For the first time in twenty-two days, I tasted coffee when he brought me a cup to comfort me.

"Sir, is there any way I can get a work visa if you release me?"

"No, you cannot. You were illegal for more than a year and therefore you have a life ban from entering or working in UAE again. But since you are here, we are going to release you so you can go to the court and remove the travel ban. Then you can come back here again.

"You know, once upon a time we Syrians were a proud nation, with dignity and respect. Things have changed so much. To use your power against the powerless is not a heroic act. Real heroes show mercy. But we are on our own. Release me, please."

An hour later, I was free to go. They gave me a piece of paper in case the police stopped me, but they held onto my passport. Surrounded by high walls in the dark, and having not been outside for a month, I realized that I had lost my sense of direction. Standing in the prison yard, I looked around, searching for the exit gate. I just wanted to get out of there but couldn't find my way.

I went up to the only guard standing in the yard. "Where is the exit gate and where is the road, please?"

"What is wrong with you? This is the exit gate, and you are standing on the road, just keep walking."

Walking along the sand road, carrying the small bag Jehad had brought me for my journey, I knew that I was only delaying what was certain—I would be back at this place I hated the most—but it felt good to smell some fresh air and enjoy what little freedom I now had. At least I could call my family now, and perhaps by the time

I was back there, the phones would be installed. You wish, said the voice in my head.

Yet again I was on the streets of Abu Dhabi, legal but not legal, with no place to go or car to sleep in. I went into a grocery and, using some of the money Solaf had sent while I was in jail, bought a coffee, cigarettes and a new charger for my phone. First I sat on a bench and did nothing but enjoy the air, the coffee and the smoke. Then I went to a restaurant, enjoyed some shawarma while my phone charged and then called my family. There were tears of relief when they heard my voice, but I did not tell them what was going on nor the reason I'd been released. Give them a break for, God's sake. Let them feel happy for a little bit—they've been through a lot too, I said to myself. "Everything is going to be all right now," I told them. "I am fine and safe, and will start looking for a job in a short time." Then I asked myself the familiar question, What next?

I would try again. Maybe I could find a job and get some money before I turned myself in again. Maybe I could find someone with the power to remove the life ban so I could get a work permit. I had heard that Sudan was accepting Syrians with just an arrival visa, so I visited their embassy to check. Half of the rumour was true—Sudan was accepting Syrians on arrival visas at that time, but only those who travelled directly from Syria, or who had a work permit in the Gulf area or for any other country. So it was not for me.

I rented a room close to Jehad, and he offered me a part-time job, one I could do from my room. We couldn't risk me being caught, as we would both be in trouble. I worked on marketing his latest project, but without being able to go out to work or drive, it felt like I was in prison again. It lasted seven months, during which time the court was going through seven years of paper records—nothing had been computerized—to find the documents relating to my travel ban. Eventually, it was lifted and I was ready to return to the immigration detention centre.

With my suitcase at my side, I tried to turn myself in eight times. I would stand next to the gate, early in the morning, only to be sent away every time by the guards. "Come after the holidays. It's Sunday. We only accept people on Tuesdays." These were some of the excuses they used until I decided enough was enough; I decided to just wait there. When the officer I had met before pulled into the yard and parked his car I went up to him and reminded him who I was.

"Here is my phone number," he said, handing me a card. "Come back anytime—Sunday, Monday or any day you want. I will let you in and I will help you to travel as soon as possible with no delay. But I need you to do something first. Go to the Malaysian Embassy and make sure that they don't want a visa from you. It will be better if you can bring me a letter from them just to make sure."

With my suitcase, I stood in front of a clerk at the Malaysian Embassy, a glass wall between us, and explained the situation. She told me that if the authorities sent them an email, they would respond, but that she couldn't give me a letter. "Would it be okay if he called, so he can hear this himself?" I asked. She was pleasant, from Sudan originally, and she also showed me an official embassy document that listed the nationalities who could enter Malaysia with an arrival visa. Syrians were listed, but she refused to give me a copy.

I called the officer from the embassy, and the lady from Sudan spoke to him. At the end of the call, the officer said, "You can come now." I took a photo of myself at the embassy, to prove I'd been there. Just in case.

Early the next day, Sunday, I was there at the gate. I sent him a text and a few minutes later he showed and escorted me in. We sat in his office and chatted a little. Before he handed me over to the guards, he promised me it would not take long, a matter of a day or two. I believed him and had to trust him—there was nothing else I could do.

It was not a day or two, it was twenty-two days, the same as my first stay at the detention centre. Nothing had changed except the place was much dirtier, so filthy that using the bathroom was like attempting suicide. Each day I stood next to the door, hoping to see the officer or to pass a message to him via one of the guards. Occasionally I saw him in the distance, and he would either wave and say, "It will not take long," before disappearing, or he would ignore me. What could I do? There was a bloody great door between us and I could hardly run after him. With every sunrise and every sunset, I regretted turning myself in again.

I had turned myself in on November 5, 2017. Eighteen days later, a Thursday, I got sick, really sick: shaking, sweating, stomach pains, vomiting. The other prisoners, noticing the state I was in, called the guards to do something. "It's Thursday evening," they said. "The doctor only comes on workdays, from Sunday to Thursday, so we can't do anything until Sunday morning. We might have some Panadol." Hearing that made me lose it, and I start shouting. I let out all the anger I felt at the indifference and carelessness and betrayal. I let it all out and no one answered.

That weekend, some kind fellow inmates sat next to me, doing whatever they could, bringing me food from the kitchen to my bed, sharing their oranges with me, keeping the cold compresses coming. They were acting like human beings who feel the pain of another. They were poor guys with nothing to gain and no future, but still they were kind and generous. We had no shared language, so they could only smile at me, smiles that said, "Forgive me that I can't do anything more to make you feel better." These were the kind of people I wished I could have as friends for life.

Shouting that Thursday evening, threatening to go on a hunger strike and start an uprising in the block, must have made some impression, because first thing Sunday morning they sent the doctor to me. While he was examining me, an officer arrived and asked if I would be okay to fly, as a flight was booked for me for the next morning. As ill as I was, this reminded me that being afraid and being weak weren't the same things. It was a lesson I first learned as a child.

"Face your fear. Don't show your weakness, and know that the ones you are facing are feeling afraid too." Those were my father's words to me when I was in Grade Five. We were working at the farm, the three of us, my father, Ammar and me. Ammar was in Grade Two, and while we both were walking, we saw a snake creeping between the rocks, black and scary. We ran to our father as quickly as we could, crying and screaming.

"Why are you crying?" he asked us.

"A snake, there is a snake, we saw a snake!" We were out of breath, as if we had run away from death itself.

"And?"

"And what?" We tried to wipe away our tears.

"Take this." My father handed me the shovel he was holding. "Now go back and find it, and don't come back unless you've killed it."

I took the shovel and Ammar and I went back to where we'd seen the snake, just like that. Our father was watching us from a distance, making sure we were okay.

On our way back home that evening, as he drove my father glanced at me and asked, "Do you know why I sent you back there?"

"No." *I am still mad at you. Don't speak to me, please.*

"The snake was afraid of you as well, and it slithered away the second it saw you, just like you did. The only time it would attack you first is when it feels your fear and smells your weakness. The best way to protect yourself is to show it that you are strong and ready for it. Remember this—face your fear, don't show your weakness, and know that the ones you are facing are feeling afraid too."

I had not fully understood my father's words then. But they came back to me at that moment in the detention centre in Abu Dhabi.

I promised myself I would not be afraid of saying the wrong thing, and that I would always speak up for myself, with pride and dignity. The next time would be in Malaysia.

Different officers, different investigators from different departments, different questions, all throughout that Sunday until they finally called my name again at around 5:00 p.m. I was exhausted, hungry and sick, both physically and emotionally, from their repeated questions.

"You are coming with us," the officers said, and with no further discussion they handcuffed me, dragged me to a police car and drove to the airport police station.

I was wearing jail clothes—an orange T-shirt, a pair of too-big shorts and flip-flops—and had to keep my elbows close to my waist to stop the shorts from falling down. All that evening, they kept me handcuffed during the two interviews I had, one with a woman from the UNHCR, and the other with a representative from the Malaysian Human Rights Directorate. The handcuffs, there to remind me of my situation, restrict my movement and break my spirit, failed in their purpose. Like the shovel my father had given me, they made me feel powerful instead. The guards and police officers who kept interrupting the meetings, peering out at us to know what we were talking about, worried that I was saying bad things about how I had been treated, they became the snakes. I looked up to the left—this time, Father, I am not going to be breathless as if I am trying to get ahead of death, this time I am going to run into my fate and face it. I will not let them feel my fear or smell my weakness. You have my word.

Chapter Six

A Normal Person

"I WON'T HANDCUFF you if you behave," said the officer who was driving me to the airport. I still felt sick, despite the heavy drugs the doctor had loaded me up with to make me fit enough to fly, so "behave" was all I could do. On the road, he started to lecture me about the political tensions in the Gulf and how the UAE and Saudi Arabia were going to take over Qatar, then Iran and when they'd finished all of that, they would take over Turkey. I was dizzy and couldn't focus, so I didn't say anything, but I did think, Yeah, you're the successor of Alexander the Great, for sure! I worried throughout the journey that something might go wrong at the last minute— would he take me back to the jail again?

My worries were partially justified. When we reached the airport police station, the officer left me in the car while he went in to organize handing responsibility for me over to them. He came back a few minutes later with the weirdest look on his face.

"I need to call my boss."

"What for? What is going on? They refused, didn't they?"

"Yes. They said you are from Syria, and if you are going to be deported, it will be to your country only. Not to Malaysia. Not to any other country."

"Don't they know international law? Don't answer that, please. Just call your boss. I paid for a ticket and he booked it for me. I am sure he knew what he was doing."

The call lasted less than a minute. The senior officer decided to come to the airport himself, the first and only time someone from law enforcement was willing to help. Without him and his assistance on that day, I would probably still be in the UAE. Individuals can make a difference if they choose to do so. He didn't bother to try to get approval from the airport police station. Instead, he smuggled me through to departures, calling in a favour from the immigration officer on duty, who was someone he'd served with and knew.

"Don't say anything," he instructed me. "Just follow me and keep your mouth shut. Try to act like a VIP, too."

VIP! That would be hard, with the way I looked. But I managed to keep my mouth shut until needed.

At the immigration desk, with the senior officer's assistant at my side, I told the man about the successful meetings I'd had in UAE, how I was going to invest a huge amount of money the next month, and wasn't it unfortunate that I'd lost my suit bag, which was why I didn't look like a VIP at that moment.

After the immigration officer stamped my passport, I went through the barrier, feeling safe, relieved my rambling explanations had worked. But before I headed to the plane, I looked back over my shoulder at the man who had helped me and waved and smiled. He waved back, sharing my victory. It was a beautiful feeling—my last memories of that country are of a friendly face, a smile and a wave, just like any other normal passenger. That experience taught me that representatives of the law can work through it, not just by the book, to get a humanitarian result. That man showed the essence and spirit of the law, not just the words and rules. The words punish, the spirit helps.

"Al Kontar. Calling Hassan Al Kontar to Gate 19." I was late, and the flight to Kuala Lumpur was being held just for me. As I ran to catch it, I called my family—the first time I'd been able to speak to them for twenty-two days—to tell them the good news. "I am at the airport now, on my way to Malaysia! Everything is behind us now, it's a new start!" It was a call full of tears, but joyous ones.

The plane was large and almost empty. As I walked down the aisle, looking for my seat, I told myself, "You are on a plane—you going to fly for the first time in ten years. You are free. And you are never going to be in jail again." The pleasure of doing something I loved, travelling by plane, overshadowed what I was not thinking about—that I was flying to a country where I didn't know anyone or how things worked. When I came to my row, there was a couple seated there.

"Sir, you are sitting in my seat," I said to the man in Arabic.

"The plane is almost empty. Sit somewhere else."

"Exactly! It's empty. I could do that, but what is so special about my seat?"

I said this with a smile, as I was feeling happy and wanted to joke. Before he could answer me, a flight attendant showed up. She was very beautiful, with short dark hair topped with a small red hat. Her uniform fit her tall figure perfectly, and mascara accented her bold eyes. She flashed a red-lipsticked smile at us all, evaluating the situation. In perfect English, she said to the man, "Sir, look at this poor guy! This is his seat."

Poor guy! You are not wrong, I wanted to say to her, but you should have seen me ten minutes ago when I was a businessman in the VIP hall.

Her first reaction and description of me—poor man—was an honest one. I certainly did not look like a tourist or even a normal passenger. Then she apologized for speaking improperly, and I said she was just being honest. "Our first reactions are the most honest and truthful feelings. Before the mind takes control." We both started to laugh. In the end, we discovered that the usurper spoke no English, was from Saudi Arabia, and that this was his first flight, a honeymoon with his new bride. So I took another window seat on a different row and asked the beautiful attendant to make it up to me by keeping the coffee coming. Which she did, although I was more interested in the beauty who was delivering it than the beverage itself.

Being alone is different from being lonely. While being alone is a matter of choice, being lonely is a sensation that becomes part of your personality, as I discovered during those years in the UAE. Loneliness becomes your destiny, and you can't get rid of it; better to learn with time not to be sad, to make your own peace with it. So we run back to our safe space, seeking comfort with ourselves and closing the door to our souls as we close the door to our room. In the outside world, we act—funny, sassy, aggressive, friendly—and we keep doing it until it's not an act anymore but who we are.

I had tried acting normal once in Abu Dhabi when I had enough money in my pocket for a beer. Let me be normal, like any other guy my age, I told myself. I decided to go to a bar, where I sat down and scanned the room: fancy place, calm music, normal people chatting and smiling. I knew that when I finished my beer, I would go back to sleep in my car. Without ordering, I stood up and left— they were normal, I was acting. In Malaysia, I decided, I was going to really be a normal person again.

Buying a SIM card for my phone, booking a hotel room, flashing my valid ID—everything felt like a privilege and made me smile. The feeling of not being followed, of not being at risk, overwhelmed me. No police or immigration officials were hunting for me. "I am safe now," I kept telling myself. I was legal—my visa was valid for three months—and I need to act fast to take advantage of my new situation and keep it that way.

I had heard stories about Malaysia, the country's economy and urban development, about the lifestyle and costs, about the possibility of work and the openness of the market. I was full of optimism and started exploring the capital the next day, focused on one thing only: find employment, get a work permit.

It was strange getting into a car with a steering wheel on the left. The weather was humid and it rained heavily, but briefly. The main streets were clean and tidy, lined with oil palm trees (the Malaysian national tree). Not far from the twin skyscrapers, the Petronas Towers, I discovered Arab Street, where Arab shops, products and food can be found. It would become a place where I would spend time in the next months.

I did not mix with the local people much, but on the few occasions I did, they seemed kind. In everything, their way of life and traditions were very different, including their food and the way they make their coffee and tea. They seemed to be open-minded and non-judgemental. To be in an Islamic country, where public shops can sell alcohol, was a sign of tolerance for me. I didn't know when I first arrived that the Malaysian population consisted of three main races—Malay, Indian and Chinese—and that their history was thorny and complex.

As I sent out my resume and attended job interviews, it did not take long for the reality I had tried to ignore to force itself on me. Finding legal work was not as easy as I had dreamed it would be. The time was short and the money was shorter, and I was too ashamed to ask my family to send me money again. As the eldest son, I was the one who was supposed to be taking care of them. They were living in a country at war, and I couldn't keep asking them to support me.

I was a stranger in a strange country, feeling both alone and lonely, walking the streets with no destination and no hope of seeing a familiar face. I'd stop at a local shop to buy a local coffee, just trying to belong, only to throw it away after the first sip. I'd look at the normal people, living and enjoying their lives, and wonder, what did I do wrong? I'd look at my watch. What time is it now? It didn't matter. And in my mind, a running commentary on my situation: You have no place to go, no work to do, no one to meet. Don't be mad at them, it's not their fault. It's just bad timing, it's not the end yet. I refuse to believe that it's the end. If I think that, then what am I supposed to do tomorrow morning? No, I will wake up tomorrow, walk again, think of a solution, keep dreaming to be like them, the normal people, while I buy a cup of local coffee to feel that I belong and throw it away again after the first sip.

But I still had hope. Hope, even if false, is a treatment for the soul—it pushes you to keep moving, to look toward the future, not back over your shoulder. Hope is why we keep on breathing, why we still get up each morning. While I was in Malaysia, I started to write new memories, to rebuild the history of my family and childhood that had been lost when I was arrested in the UAE. I no longer had the souvenirs, letters, documents and photos to touch and read to remind me of home and I wanted something to show my sons in the future, as my father had shown me his papers when I asked him. Another gesture of hope.

Six weeks after I arrived in Malaysia, I received an email, a response to one of the hundreds I had sent out with my resume attached. Could this be my hope, my dream of a new start, fulfilled? I googled the company, and its website seemed legit. I trimmed my hair and beard, polished my shoes and put on a new tie—I was going to look like the professional I had once been. Carrying a file with a hard copy of my resume, I went to the address and rode the elevator to the fourteenth floor. There was a security desk at the main entrance office, and I introduced myself, explaining I had an interview. They gave me a visitor card on a lanyard, which I hung around my neck, and I went into the beautiful foyer. I sat next to a Christmas tree in the corner of the reception area and waited to be called.

A man came and escorted me to a meeting room with a large screen on one wall. He explained that the company's owner was a Malaysian woman who was out of the country on important business. "She will interview you via Skype," he told me and set up the call. Throughout the interview, only half her face showed on the screen, which I thought was strange. Because this was my first, my only, opportunity, I couldn't let myself be suspicious or doubt what she was saying. Keeping my hope alive, I decided it was probably just a technical issue. The interview was a short one, and she ended it by telling me she was going to make me her general manager. The salary she was offering was huge. Aren't you too young, with no local experience, to be a general manager? I asked myself, but I pushed the doubt away and decided to believe her. Afterwards, I called my family to tell them the good news. "I keep reading on social media about magical stories and wonderful coincidences happening to other people all over the world. It changes their lives, so why not me too? Maybe it's finally happening for me!" I said to Solaf, after telling her about the official job offer.

She was doubtful. "Maybe it's happening to other people, but not for us. We are on our own."

It took me three working days—waking up each morning at 6:00 a.m. to catch the train, wearing my new tie and thinking of buying a new one (not cool for a general manager to wear the same tie every day), coming back at 8:00 p.m.—three full days to discover it was a scam. The Malaysian businesswoman was actually wanted for a number of crimes and she was just using me as the frontman for her latest scam. The fact that she made me pay 200 ringgit (about $50) for the security card I needed to enter the office should have warned me. I'm educated, consider myself smart, but hope made me stupid. Hope made me believe when all the evidence was there that the dream job was just another fraud.

The reality that I tried to ignore and forget forced itself on me.

I had thought that getting a job would be the route to getting a work visa and the right to stay in the country, but a Syrian man I met on Arab Street explained to me how wrong I was. I learned that even if I found a legitimate job, the immigration department would not authorize work permits for Syrian citizens. If you are wealthy and are going to invest in the country, Malaysia has a program that offers residency for foreigners. My only way to stay in Malaysia legally after my three-month visitor visa expired would be to obtain a study visa, which would cost thousands of dollars I did not have. Off-grid work, with a salary barely enough to pay the rent, was a possibility, but the spectre of those long years in the UAE chilled me. I didn't want to be homeless, jobless and hunted again. There was another alternative—register with the local government program for refugees—but this I would not consider. In the UAE I was an illegal but I never identified myself as a refugee. The Malaysian refugee program is not recognized by other counties or international organizations, and if you register, you cannot apply for employment or obtain a residency or work permit. I believed this program was designed only to allow Malaysia to defend itself to the international community and human rights organizations.

So my priority shifted from employment to legal status. I didn't want to stay in a country where I could not be a legal resident. As a Syrian, where could I go and how would I get there? After the war started, Syrians had to become experts in international law and the methods of seeking asylum: which countries were party to the 1951 Refugee Convention and which, like Malaysia, were not. Syrians had to know which airlines would allow us to board or not, which airports we could use. Traffickers, people smuggling, landline routes, fake passport rings and who controls them and the cost of escape—all this knowledge was the new reality for Syrians. Since the war began, we discovered a new kind of racism against us, as international powers used the war for their own agenda, and the Syrian people became tools to achieve their goals. For us, discrimination was no longer just about skin colour, religion and gender, it was geographical and nationalist racism. Being a Syrian means that the world is closed to you, regardless of your humanity or who you are as an individual. It is not enough that they close the door, they have to justify why they do it—Syrians are portrayed as ignorant terrorists, dirty people living in tents who are uneducated and unskilled, not the victims of war, violence and terrorism.

Now that I knew I had to leave Malaysia, I had no choice but to go back to my family for money. Letting them down again was painful, but I knew there was no other answer and that they would understand. They did.

It took them some time to get together the money I would need to get out of Malaysia. As both my parents had been government employees, they continued to receive a pension after their retirement, even during the war. My family had some savings as well, but inflation was rampant and some things were just not available anymore. But I believe people adapt to their new reality to survive. Solaf and my mother sold their gold necklaces and raised $3000. Getting it out of Syria to me was another challenge, as international money transfers were forbidden.

They found a man in Sweida who had a brother living and working in Kuwait. That brother agreed to send me the $3000 from his account, and my mother paid the man in Sweida the money. How the two brothers later sorted it out, I don't know. By the time the money finally arrived, I had already overstayed my visa by six weeks, but I went straight to the immigration department. I knew that they would stamp my passport with a ban from entering Malaysia for five years, but that did not matter. I wanted out, so I paid the fine, accepted the ban and was given fifteen days to leave the country legally.

I thought about it carefully, I calculated all the risks, researched and checked everything, and finally decided on my destination:

Ecuador, one of only a handful of countries that would allow Syrians to land with just an arrival visa. What I was going to do there, I had no idea. They don't even speak English and I would know no one. None of that mattered. I just wanted a place where I could be legal. I would figure out everything else later.

Like other Syrian travel experts, I decided to avoid all European airlines and airports, even as a transit stop. A European airline might not let me board the flight if they knew I was going through a European airport. They might question my real intentions and assume I would try to stay and seek asylum the moment we touched down. So, it had to be Turkish Airlines, with a flight from Kuala Lumpur through Istanbul and then on to Bogota. In Bogota, I would change to Avianca Airlines to fly to Quito, the capital of Ecuador. A fifty-two-hour flight, but a safe one. I was desperate and didn't want to raise any suspicions. So before I booked the airline tickets, I went to the Turkish Embassy in Kuala Lumpur and to the head office of Turkish Airlines to confirm that a transit visa wasn't needed to travel through Istanbul. I also went to the Colombian Embassy to confirm the same, if a transit visa was needed to change planes in Bogota.

When confirmed that I was good to go, I booked the tickets and told myself this was going to work. I planned it well—why wouldn't it work? I had both return tickets as required, a valid passport with more than six months left on it, some cash and a hotel reservation, just like any other tourist. Ecuador allowed Syrians to enter the country for three months with an arrival visa. Once I was there, I planned to apply for asylum, as Ecuador is a signatory of the Refugee Convention. The tickets cost me almost $2000, leaving me with $800 after the fine I'd paid for overstaying.

It was almost sunset when I called a taxi and headed to Kuala Lumpur Airport's Terminal 1 with a bag containing my clothes and my new memories. The airport was forty minutes away, and the driver only asked me where I was from and where I was going. For the rest of the journey, there was just silence mixed with anticipation, caution and fear, feelings that Syrians have become familiar with whenever they are about to travel. For most people, airports are happy places related to holidays or business trips, a portal to new places and cultures. For some, it's routine, like using a bus or a train, but not for us, not for a Syrian like me—the airport was the last doorway between life and death, freedom or jail. The airline employee who takes your bags and hands you your boarding pass, the immigration officer with the stamp in his hand, they both might change your life forever. Their mood—are they having a good day or a bad one?—could change your destiny.

The Turkish Airlines' check-in counter was staffed by a Malaysian woman, their local employee. She asked for my passport and ticket and I handed them over. She examined both and then referred to her system monitor.

"Sir, I need your return ticket, please."

"Here you are."

"Sir, you have a bag. We can't accept it."

"Why not?"

"There is no agreement between us and Avianca Airlines. Your bag will not be transferred to their plane at Bogota airport.

"Okay. I will carry it as hand luggage. This the only bag I have."

"No, sir. This is too big for carry-on luggage."

"Okay, what do you want me to do? Throw it away?"

"I don't know, sir, but we can't have it on board."

"Fine. I will be back."

If the bag was the only thing standing between me and being legal, with no more jails and running, then it was not a hard choice. The bag would go. It was not the first time I lost some belongings and memories. I went to the toilet, and there was a man cleaning the floor. I called him over, opened the bag and showed him the clothes and other stuff.

"Take it. It's yours," I said left.

I went back to the line of passengers at the check-in desk and waited my turn. The Malaysian woman saw me and called me up to the desk.

"Do you have money and a hotel reservation?"

"Yes, I do."

"Can I see them?"

"Sure. Is everything okay? Do you normally ask all these questions of other passengers from other nationalities?"

Before she could answer, a chubby Turkish man in his mid-forties with a two-day stubble on his chin and prescription glasses came up behind her at the counter. The ID card hanging from his neck said "Supervisor" and he looked like the kind of man impressed with himself and his job title. Without greeting me or even giving me a proper look, he took my documents and began to check them. He pointed his finger at the waiting line behind me. That finger and the hand that was waving it were telling me to go back to the end of the line and wait there. So I did, and I waited.

With that wave of his hand, I feared my careful plans were not going to work, but I refused to let hope go. I couldn't understand why he wouldn't let me go, there seemed no logic behind it and desperate thoughts ran through my mind: He must let me go! I've paid all my money! I only have a week left on my fifteen-day extension visa! I have no other place to go! What I am supposed to tell my family waiting for my call? That I failed you again?

It seemed that this was something personal between him and me. Why was he avoiding any eye contact and refusing to answer any of my questions? The other passengers were passing by me, almost through me, their shoulders brushing against mine as they checked in, got their boarding passes and headed toward the plane in a matter of minutes. But not me. I watched him confirm all the other passengers, including those on the standby list.

On March 1, 2018, at around 9:00 p.m., after two hours of waiting and being ignored, my questions unanswered, the supervisor refused to allow me to board. The air went dark, so dark that I could not see where I was or who was near me. In that darkness, I forgot the danger I was putting myself into when I started to shout, police surrounding me.

I never knew his name, but his face will always be there, representing humanity in its ugliest form. He did not even have the courage to give me back my passport in person and explain why he had made his decision. He sent the Malaysian woman out with it.

She gave me my passport with only one sentence: "Sorry, sir. You are not allowed to board."

That "sir" was more mocking than respectful. There was no respect in what they had done.

I pulled out my phone and tracked the supervisor moving behind the check-in counters. It was the first time I had ever filmed anyone and I think perhaps it was my subconscious telling me to gather the evidence I would need in my fight. Or maybe I was just trying to make him feel afraid, or at least worry about the consequences of his decision.

My body trembled as I stumbled along, still filming him. Then, with a voice trying to show strength not emotion, I called out a question to him that was a turning point for me, one that would change the way I thought forever and would determine my future course of action. "Would you do the same if I was holding an American, Canadian, Australian or European passport?"

He didn't answer. He didn't have to. Before I left the airport, after threatening him with using the video, I asked him one more question: "How can your government claim that it is a friend of the Syrian people, while one of its employees is nothing but a hater and racist toward us?"

I was not asking him these questions expecting an answer from

111

him. I was asking them to find comfort in who I am. I wanted to shout out so loud that my heart and soul could hear. This was not my fault!

I understood at that moment how someone could commit murder—the rage at being powerless in the face of injustice. At that moment, if I had been holding a gun, I might have done something I never thought myself capable of, to prove that I was *not* powerless and they were *wrong*. Pulling the trigger might have extinguished the volcano inside.

I exited the airport's main door, facing passengers who were happily hurrying in with their bags to catch their planes. Me, I was moving in the opposite direction. At the outside smoking zone, I lit up a cigarette and called my family, lying to them yet again: "No worries, a small problem. I need to change my ticket and the airline." They knew it had to be something bigger, but they did not ask too many questions.

There was no time to brood over what had happened. I needed to come up with another plan and grieve for the failed one later. Life seemed to be taking every opportunity to smack me down.

My only hope was to try a different airline, travelling via a European airport. The next day, the travel agency refused to refund my money and offered to issue me a new ticket for the same route, with added fees. That would have been a waste of both time and money, as there was no reason to think that the supervisor would act differently on another day. I went to the Turkish Embassy and the Turkish Airlines office to complain, but they refused to listen. I sent an email to the airline's headquarters, and they replied with a complaint file number and a promise to investigate. That was the last I heard from them.

I was obsessed with finding a place where I would not be an illegal. On the final day of my fifteen-day extension, I went to a travel agency early in the morning to book a flight to the only country left on the map open to a Syrian, Cambodia. It was March 7, 2018, and I had $500 left in my pocket as I went back to Kuala Lumpur International Airport with a ticket for Phnom Penh.

What did I know about Cambodia anyway? I remembered Angelina Jolie in *Tomb Raider*. Was *Anna and the King* in Cambodia? Or was it Nepal?" Silly thoughts, anything to distract me from thinking about what was going to happen next.

This time I was going to KLIA2, the terminal used by Air Asia and other low-cost airlines, for destinations in Asian countries only. It will work this time, I told myself.

At the immigration desk, the Malaysian officer stamped my passport: "You can't come back for the next five years."

"I got that, but let me get on the plane, please."

From the small window I could see the clouds. I was in my favourite place, living my childhood dream, on a plane to a new country. The flight attendant was selling coffee and I bought one. As I sipped, I asked myself: "What I am doing? Does it matter if it is Ecuador or Cambodia? I don't know either, I don't speak the languages, and the only thing they have in common is that I can go there with a visitor's visa." That's when I realized that my "plans" were really just an escape with no long-term victory guaranteed. An old saying came into my mind: "Half solution is not the solution; half the truth is not the truth; half a dream is not the dream; if you decide to speak, say it all until you finish, or don't start at all."

As we approached Phnom Penh, the poverty was evident from above: houses with sheet metal roofs, what looked like slums extending for miles. As the plane landed, I remembered Damascus, the city that Mark Twain had described as the "Pearl of the East, the pride of Syria, the fabled garden of Eden, the home of princes and genii of the Arabian Nights, the oldest metropolis on Earth, the only city in all the world that has kept its name and held its place and looked serenely on while the Kingdoms and Empires of four thousand years have risen to life, enjoyed their little season of pride and pomp, and then vanished and been forgotten." The plane taxied to the gate, and a wave of nostalgia swept over me. I wanted to cry. It's not the time for poetry and romance, I told myself fiercely. First things first. Deal with the Cambodian authorities, then you can stop and do whatever you want.

The Cambodian airport was basic, not sleek and modern, with limited facilities. I passed through corridors in semi-darkness and came to a hall where there was a table with forms that needed to be completed before you got into line to see an immigration officer. I didn't know what I was doing—all I wanted was to rush through this, get out of the airport and feel safe, even if only temporarily. So I copied the other passengers, not asking any questions of the airport staff, and trying not to draw attention to myself. The smell of cigarette smoke, the officials shouting—the atmosphere was intimidating rather than welcoming. "Like a police station in Syria," I muttered to myself. I'd picked up one of the forms and was waiting in line when an officer came out of nowhere and asked for my passport and papers.

He pulled me out of the queue and scanned my passport.

"Hmmm, Syria! Follow me."

"Where to, Officer?"

The man moved quickly and I could barely keep up with him, no time for more questions, as I followed him to a glass cubicle with other officials inside, all going through the arrivals forms. One of them looked at me and asked: "Why you are here?"

"Tourism."

"For how long?"

"I think about a week, although your law allows me a month."

"Do you have money?"

"I have $500 and a credit card, of course." The card was a lie, as was the hotel reservation.

He looked at me again and said, "No, you are not allowed. We are sending you back." He handed my documents to the same officer who'd pulled me out of the line.

"Just follow me," he said, and without waiting for me he started walking. I was still trying to argue with the officer who rejected me while my eyes followed the officer retreating with my passport.

I was getting no response from the man behind the glass, so I went after the officer with my documents. He stopped suddenly in the middle of the waiting hall, and the other passengers stared at us, clearly wondering, Who is this guy and what has he done? Is he a criminal or a terrorist? How was such a man allowed to fly with us? Their eyes said it all. The officer made me face the wall, took his cellphone out of his pocket and took two photos of me, full face and profile, just like in a TV program when they arrest a criminal. I'd promised myself that was never going to happen to me again.

"What is my crime now?"

As he ignored my question, I smiled and kept on talking, looking at his face and seeing the closing scene of the tragic movie of my life—"The End"—playing across his features. We started walking again, and I asked him the same question I'd asked the Turkish Airlines supervisor, "Would you do the same if I were holding a US, Canadian or European passport?"

I would never hold my Syrian passport again.

While we were walking toward the same plane I'd arrived on, a terrible pain flashed through me, and my legs gave out—an adrenaline rush? I stopped, leaned against the wall and collapsed. I just sat there on the floor in the dim corridor, refusing to believe what just happened, trying again to find some kind of logic, but I could not. There should be a reason behind everything, and there should be a purpose for everything that exists. What is it? Where is it? I just wanted to know! But I could not find an answer. I looked up, full of anger, my eyes wide, hardly able to breathe. I bit my finger so I wouldn't shout and lose control. I wanted to feel the pain so that it would wake me up, so I wouldn't make a mistake that would make me a real criminal. I looked up at the officer and said, "This is too much, too much."

It took the Cambodian authorities less than forty-five minutes to reject me and send me back to Malaysia on the same day, on the same plane. Just like that, easy job for them, just another working day: He is someone else's problem now, and they will deal with him. On the plane, while we were making our way back through the clouds (my favourite place, my oldest dream), the flight attendant came and offered me a coffee. "Sure, why not? Let me have one, maybe it will be my last."

Back in Malaysia, at Kuala Lumpur International Airport Terminal 2, I was a man with no other place on Earth to go but Syria. I had tried every possible plan and none had worked. They worked for others, but not me, for reasons I could not understand. Life was giving me a final test, the hardest one of all.

Part Two
@THE_AIRPORT

Chapter Seven

@kontar81

AFTER THE AIRPLANE landed back at KLIA2, I did exactly as I had done at Phnom Penh, followed the man who was holding my passport and who allowed no questions. The problem I was facing was so huge I couldn't comprehend it. My mind switched off and I followed the official, terrified. Was he taking me straight to jail? What did I have to do to get people to leave me alone? How could I prove to this world that I am not a bad person? What could I say to make them understand that it was not my fault that my country was at war? I thought of my father. I had let him down, but he was in a peaceful place where he could rest. I could use some peace and rest right now, I thought.

"I hope your jail is better than the one in the Emirates," I said to the man with my passport as I followed him through gates and glass doors. He didn't respond. Once again everyone was heading one way toward their departure gates and their planes, and I was moving in the opposite direction.

It took about three minutes to reach what looked like a customer service desk. Three employees, two women and a man, sat behind a glass window that separated them from the passengers. In front of the office were some chairs, filled with waiting people. The man handed my passport to one of the women. She flipped through its pages and said, "You have been deported from Cambodia."

I had no idea what to do, was afraid I was going to end up in jail, and this was not the moment for sarcasm or jokes.

"Deported! How can I be deported from a country I never even entered in the first place?"

She smiled at me and said, "Still, you are considered as being deported."

"What should I do now?"

"Well, you have a five-year travel ban, so you can't enter Malaysia. Even if you didn't have one, we can't let you in as you are a deportee from another country."

"So what should I do?" I asked her again. I knew what she was going to say so I decided to preempt her before she could answer. "I am from Syria. I can't go there. It's a war zone." It was a long shot, and I said it in hope rather than expectation.

"Not my problem," she said. "Bring me a ticket to Syria. In the meantime, we will hold your passport."

"It will take me some time to get one," I said, stalling. "There is no direct flight to Syria. You have to travel via Lebanon, and I need a visa to enter that country. But I will try."

"Fine," she said. "You can sit on one of those seats and start working on it." Clearly, she was used to this kind of situation and this is how she handled it.

I sat down on one of the chairs and met two Egyptian guys who had been deported from South Korea and had been at KLIA2 for five days. We bonded. They had no money, so I gave one of them a few dollars and he went upstairs and brought back three big cups of coffee. The other one took me to where he normally smoked, a public toilet not far from where we sat, and together we smoked our cigarettes and drank our coffees. I was ridiculously happy at not spending the night in jail, and their presence made me feel better. They cracked jokes with their best Egyptian sense of humour, gave me a blanket—one of those thin red ones you get on an airplane that doesn't keep you warm—and showed me where I could sleep on the floor. There were armrests between each chair in the row, designed to make sleeping there a challenge. I decided not to call my family—they'd had enough grief from me, and I was going to solve this myself. How, I didn't know.

At about 2:00 a.m., two police officers came to question me for the first time.

"What are you doing here? What is your plan?"

"I am working on getting another ticket." They didn't ask where to.

"How long will it take?"

The Egyptians had been there for five days, so I said, "It will be a week, possibly." That seemed a reasonable amount of time.

When I closed my eyes that night, feeling the cold floor under me through the blanket and with a rolled-up newspaper as a pillow, I wondered what tomorrow was going to bring. Not for a moment did I imagine this place would be my home for the next seven months. I only slept for an hour or so before waking up and exploring. Two long corridors, with bathrooms at each end, ran out from either side of the central area housing the customer service office. Along each corridor were large glass windows through which you could see the runway and the planes arriving and departing; spaced along the length were seating sections and potted plants. Moving walkways ran through them. Some escalators and elevators led to the floor above, where there was the security/immigration gate that you had to pass through to enter the levels with duty-free shops and cafés.

During the day, the immigration officers and customer service staff demanded to know about my progress in getting a ticket to Damascus. I told them I was working on getting the visa to transit through Lebanon and trying to arrange the flight to Syria, but I was just trying to buy myself some time. The officials were aggressive and suspicious, and I'd known from the first morning that there was no way to get them on my side. I argued with them about the situation in Syria and international law and how I couldn't go back there. After three days, they finally agreed to the idea of deporting me to a third country, on one condition—I get a valid visa. It was clear they only agreed because they thought that, as a Syrian stuck at their airport, it would be impossible for me to do so.

At night they would come in pairs, usually between midnight and 2:00 a.m. when there were no passengers around. If I was sleeping they'd wake me up and make me sit on one of the chairs. The IDs that hung from their necks showed they were from different departments—police, immigration, airport security, intelligence, customer services—and they all asked the same questions. They were not decision-makers, just low-ranking employees who were required to report daily on those who remained at the airport and why they were still there.

I sent emails to NGOs around the world, to all the international embassies in Malaysia, to governments and presidents and kings and public figures. I sent emails to everyone I could think of in the Arab world: parliament members, ministers, sheikhs. They all ignored me. I even applied to the Malaysian authorities, despite the five-year ban imposed on me. The Ecuador Embassy in Kuala Lumpur replied to my request for an email from them confirming that Syrians could enter their country on an arrival visa for three months. They refused—"We are not going to deal with a man stuck at the airport just because he once bought a ticket to Ecuador. This conversation is over. Contact us no more."—but at least they responded, which was enough to encourage me to keep on fighting. It was proof that I still existed as a person. Most western embassies replied with "sorry" and the suggestion that I contact the UNHCR.

I emailed the UNHCR twice but received no reply. I kept calling them, but only got a recorded message. Finally, on another try, a woman picked up. "Sorry. We can't do anything. We advise you to turn yourself in to the airport authorities."

But we all knew what the Malaysian authorities would do—force me to buy a ticket to Damascus and deport me back to Syria, or lock me up in prison.

"Sorry? We are the reason your organization exists! We are the ones you should be helping!"

"Sorry. We have no authority, and we don't have access to you at the airport."

Researching on the internet, I read about an island in the Caribbean called Montserrat, a British overseas territory. Its government had an online visa application form, which I completed. I knew it wouldn't be successful, but it helped with the Malaysian immigration people, as I could show them proof that I'd applied and was just waiting for the visa to be approved so I could book a ticket and get out of there.

In my heart, I knew none of this was going to work, but I couldn't give up hope, as that would mean the end. Things could be worse, I told myself. I could be in jail now, at least here I have my cellphone and the internet—surely, someone I'm reaching out to will help.

I didn't feel hungry. If there was food, I would eat—the staff put an airline meal in front of me three times a day: 6:00 a.m., 12 noon and 5:00 p.m. It was always the same, chicken and rice with plastic cutlery. Air Asia was responsible for me, as they had allowed me to board the flight to Cambodia in the first place and I was still officially their passenger. As long as I remained where I was, I was partially their problem. I watched the planes landing and taking off, the disembarking passengers passing by me without seeing me. On the other side of the glass that separated the arrivals corridor from the departures area, I watched the blur of people moving happily toward their departure gates. Airport staff moved around me: cleaners, security officers, airline employees.

I knew I smelled because I hadn't showered in a week, but that didn't bother my companions, the two Egyptians—they had their own aroma of fear and desperation. It was their last night at KLIA2, as both had tickets for a flight back home the next day. I was happy for them but sad that I was going to be left alone. We were sitting in silence—it was after midnight—when I asked them:

"Do either of you know Amal Donqol?"

"Who? No. Who is he?"

"He's a famous poet, from your country. Egyptian, like you."

"Poet? Really. Do you think this is the right time for poetry?"

"It's exactly the perfect time," I replied.

> *Glory to Satan, idol of the winds*
> *Who said no in the face of those who said yes*
> *who taught humans to tear apart nothingness*
> *He who said no, yet did not die*
> *And remained an eternal pain soul*
> *I am hanging on the gallows of the morning*
> *My forehead bowed by death*
> *Because I did not bow to her alive*[1]

For three days, days in which I thought about rebelling and revolutions, Donqol's words had refused to leave me alone. I'd been trying for a realistic solution, one that was compatible with The System. To The System, I was a deportee returned from Cambodia, and as a deportee there was only one option, return to my home country.

When we think of revolutions or rebellions, the images of armed

---

[1] My translation from "Spartacus' Last Words" by Amal Donqol

struggle, civil disobedience, coups and demonstrations come to mind. The overthrowing of dictatorial rule conjures up the faces of men like Gandhi, Guevara, Mandela, King. But for me, all these men began with one simple word: NO. We Syrians know very well about saying no; it is in our blood and our history. In the Third Century CE, Zenobia, the queen of Palmyra, said no to the Roman Empire and created a powerful independent kingdom for decades until the Romans conquered her. We all remember Zenobia, but not the names of the men who laid siege to Palmyra.

The words from another poem, one by a famous contemporary Syrian poet, also ran through my head:

> *Not to choose is cowardice,*
> *There is no middle ground,*
> *Between Heaven and Hell.*[2]

Every night I sat in silence, observing the activity on the other side of the glass, waiting for the next aggressive and intimidating visit from the police. That silence was echoed by the silence from all the people and organizations I had reached out to for help. My voice was not heard. I looked up to my left, for my father's face, while poetry, lyrics and dramatic speeches from novels, films and television, came to me over and over again. The faces of the people I had missed and lost because of the war haunted me. This airport was my middle ground—I needed to choose. Those words and faces helped me in that silent corridor. No. I chose no. One last battle.

This airport was the battlefield, the place where my life would be decided forever. I could hear the voice of *Game of Thrones'* Tyrion Lannister saying, "Are you afraid? Good. You're in the great game now. And the great game's terrifying." My own voice rang through my head. I have been running for years. I have lost so many battles,

---

[2] My translation from "Choose" by Nizar Qabbani

withdrawn from too many. But this is it, this is my last one, and I am not going to run this time. So many mistakes, but this is the time to do the right thing and correct them all.

What I was about to do was terrifying, and I would probably fail and lose this final battle, but I was going to make that silent world hear me. I was going to tell the story I had to tell. Not my personal one, but the story of Syrians. I felt the weight of it and the duty calling me. For years, I had done nothing for those who were dying because of the war, for those who were living in refugee camps, desperate to be heard. Now was the time to be their voice, their spokesman. With my headphones in my ears, holding a cup of coffee I'd had to bribe an airport cleaner to buy for me from the Starbucks outside the barrier, I taunted this life as it had taunted me: Fine. You want to play? Let us play, no more realistic solutions, no more safe escape plans. It will be American style this time. Let's make some noise.

How was I going to play the great game? The airport wi-fi gave me internet access and I had my cellphone. It was going to be my weapon.

In the past, I rarely used social media, just a Facebook account for my family and friends back in Syria. During my illegal years, my account was dormant, and I only began to post on Facebook again when I went to Malaysia. The first post I shared was the view from my window seat on the flight to Kuala Lumpur the previous October. In the UAE, I'd created a fake Instagram to set up my solar panel installation business that made me some money for a while. I'd never used Twitter, but I believed that it was more serious than Instagram and Facebook. It was where social and political dialogue happened, so it was where I was going to start. More importantly, my family only used Facebook and I didn't want them to know about my situation. Naively, I thought that I would solve the problem first and then tell them. Also naively, I thought I could control social media. If I didn't use Facebook, I could control what my family did or did not see. I really believed I could hide it from them.

Should I write a tweet or record a video? What is it going to be about? What should I say? Where should I film it? Do I need to be serious, angry and complaining, or just be my smiling self? I had no experience of how to handle these platforms and what would work best. I needed a strategy, like one of the marketing plans I used to come up with for the insurance business. Whatever I came up with, whatever I was going to write or film, it had to be based on five principles: this was a humanitarian story, not a political or religious one; it was not only my personal story, it was the story of my people; I was to explain, not complain; I wasn't selling my story, I was telling it; and, finally, whatever I delivered would be without tears—statements with a smile.

The video I tweeted was in Arabic and recorded more than ten times before I posted it, I wanted it to be right and to present my five core ideas. On March 11, 2018, @kontar81 tweeted for the first time:

إسمي حسان القنطار، أنا من سوريا، كما ترون أنا موجود في مطار كوالالمبور الدولي، ماليزيا، المبنى رقم ٢، وأنا عالق هنا. لايسمحون لي بالدخول.
أريد فقط ان أشرح للناس ما الذي يعنيه أن تكون سوريا؟ كيف تبدو؟ وما هو شعورك؟
هي أن تشعر بانك وحيد، ضعيف، مرفوض، لا أحد يقبل بك

> What does it mean to be a Syrian? My name is Hassan and this is my story. I am from Syria. I just want to explain to people what it means to be Syrian. To be lonely, weak, unwanted, rejected. No one is accepting us.

Let me double my chances, I said to myself and signed up for an Instagram account. I recorded an English language version of my video and as Kontar_81 posted both, divided into parts because of the sixty-second limit for videos on that platform. Neither was very good.

Nobody liked, nobody commented, nobody followed, nobody messaged, nobody retweeted. @kontar81 and kontar_81 did not trend. Days passed, but I kept on trying. The only alternative was detention jail and a ticket to Damascus. It was frustrating not to understand how social media worked. How could silly pranks and naked dancing be a trend and not the real story of a serious situation?

I asked myself, what if it was me who was watching? What would get my attention? What would make it interesting? I wasn't going to be another crying guy, nagging all the time and attacking others. People had their own problems, their own issues. If all I showed was negativity, they would avoid viewing and reading, because there was nothing they could do. That's how I would probably respond myself. What I needed to do was show people, before they started their day or headed out to work, that things could be worse—you could be me stuck at the airport. What I needed to do was to show them positivity, to make them smile before they started their day, to value the small things they had in life and to take nothing for granted. I would be myself, someone who came close to giving up, but didn't. I needed to be creative.

Creativity was also required to make existing in this airport limbo bearable; the skills and knowledge I acquired during my imprisonment and time as an illegal in the UAE were going to help get me through. Small, everyday problems can become major ones when you're forced to live the way I had in the Emirates, and now I was facing them again in KLIA2.

How to keep myself clean? How to take a shower when there are no showers? How to wash my clothes? Where to dry them? It's an airport, I can't just hang out my underwear in front of agents and passengers. What should I do if I get hungry? What to do if the food they give me isn't enough? How to get my coffee? When to sleep? Where to sleep?

Problems may seem unsolvable, but every problem has a key, and all you need to do is to think about the key, not the problem itself. Once you find it and work out how to use it, then what was a problem just becomes your normal daily routine.

The answer was in the word "routine." I needed to study the airport's daily routine to establish my own. What time do the police switch shifts? When do the cleaning staff come in the morning? What are the different uniforms, and who do they belong to? When are the busiest hours? The slowest? How many toilets can I access? What's there that I can use? Who can I make friends with among the staff? And what will it cost me? Where are the best spots for wi-fi access? Which areas are covered by security cameras and which are not? Where are the darkest places, and where are the quietest ones? Where can I find some privacy?

Clean clothes: use the cleaning staff. I would pay them to take my clothes home, wash them and bring them back. I'd observe and work out the best people to approach.

Washing: use the disabled toilet—it's bigger with fewer people going there. Make sure it's after 1:00 a.m. when no planes arrive for three hours.

Sleeping: the spot under the escalator. I could use the yellow barriers they put up for maintenance as walls, and they would give me a bit of privacy while I slept. The time to sleep was between 1:30 a.m. and 4:00 a.m. when the flight from China arrived.

There were no cameras in the toilets and one small room at the end of the corridor. That room, however, had no wi-fi and was next to the airport's detention area, so it would be better to avoid it.

The immigration office had an old coffee machine, but it rarely worked properly, so I decided to use the coffee machine next to the police office.

Right! All set. But I still needed someone to help me with food and better coffee. I needed someone who had access to the outside to get me things I might need. One cleaner caught my attention and seemed a likely candidate. Krishna was a slim man in his mid-thirties, although he looked younger, and he wore three silver rings on each hand and a heavy silver chain around his neck. He claimed they were all gifts from his many girlfriends, but his explanations changed whenever I asked, as if he was inventing a new story each time. With his top shirt buttons undone and his oily hair, he had the air of a Don Juan, and he bullied his co-workers. He was clearly cleverer and he acted like their boss, even though he wasn't. He'd convinced them that he spoke English, although he didn't, and he was ready to take advantage of any opportunity to make extra money. He could be funny and was helpful if you paid him. He knew everything about the arrivals hall and how things worked there. Krishna was the type of guy who might have achieved something with his life if he'd had a better education and someone to guide him.

The staff would turn a blind eye when they smelled cigarettes because most of them smoked in the same bathroom I used, but Krishna was the only one who would join me for a smoke. His presence made me feel more secure, and his was the only name I ever learned. Krishna was the only employee at the airport with whom I developed a relationship.

It took me a full day to teach him what "Starbucks" and "McDonald's" meant. It was the coffee I cared about. I'm not a fan of fast food, or food in general, although I do enjoy cooking for others. In the end, I downloaded the logos of both and then sent them to him via WhatsApp, along with a floor plan of upstairs, so I could show him where they were located. I wrote down what I wanted on a piece of paper and sent him upstairs. He worked it out. His purchase runs became routine and a Big Mac meal was a change from the same airline dinner the flight attendants were giving me every day. He didn't understand about straws, however, and would bring me coffee sticks instead for my drink. I ended up with a lot of coffee sticks and no straws. Krishna charged me double for the service, and as I began to run out of money I would end up downloading a photo of a jar of Nescafe so he could buy me some. I could make myself coffee using the hot water in the office and would forget about the extra food. Later, I asked him to train two other cleaners, in case he was off sick or absent. It turned out to have been a good idea because shortly after he had a bike accident while drunk and didn't show up at the airport for a month.

I found the keys, solved the problems, and dealing with them stopped taking up so much of my time that I couldn't focus on the major battle I was trying to fight. But even as I found ways to deal with the practicalities of life, I had to keep reminding myself that this was not normal, because if I accepted it as normal, then the airport would become my home. My goal was to get out of there, not to make a comfortable life there.

In my tweets (all in Arabic), I tagged celebrities like Cristiano Ronaldo and football teams popular in Arab countries (Real Madrid, Barcelona). Of course they had nothing to do with me, but I wanted to attach my tweets to popular trends, to try to draw attention to them. I tried everything I could think of to make my tweets more prominent.

> #syrian_stuck_airport #mystory_Hassan #airport_is_my_
> home #the_terminal_movie @JustinTrudeau @tomhanks
> @guardian @AP @TIME @washingtonpost@nytimes
> @RT_Erdogan @SophieT @Maisie_Williams
> @liamcunningham1 @IAMLenaHeadey @nikolajcw
> @FoxNews @cnni @ABC @TheSun

I made more videos, with jokes about coffee and food, but always explaining my story and what it means to be a Syrian: unwanted, rejected, alone, despised, victims of racism not because of who we are as individuals, but because of our nationality. It took fifteen days, but a trickle of reactions began to appear in my social media feeds, mostly from supportive individuals, but nothing from NGOs or governments, the people who had the power to help.

Syrian public figures, even those belonging to the opposition, ignored my story, probably for political reasons—they did not want to be attacked—with only one exception. Zeina Yazigi is a well-known journalist who'd been the host of a political news show on Sky News Arabia. Respected, dignified, smart, charismatic and, most importantly, caring, she is also the wife of one of Syria's most famous actors. Madame Zeina reached out to me, not as a journalist but as a human being. She didn't ask for an interview, but followed me and began retweeting my tweets. She took one of my early Arabic videos, added subtitles in English and sent it back to me. "Consider me your sister," she said. "I know you've been there a long time and you may need money, please let me help." I thanked her and promised to ask for her help financially if I needed it, but I never did. It was not about money anymore. She was the first to advise me not to pay attention to comments and to keep focusing on my message.

Under the yellow lights of the perpetually lit corridor, I tried to sleep with that thin red blanket under me; during those post-midnight hours, the voice of that mocking Other Hassan echoed in my dreams. I imagined him sitting next to me, well turned out as always, clean and smelling good, with a sharp suit and tie and a briefcase by his side.

"Why?" I asked him.

"You know why!"

"No, I don't. Why?"

"How stupid are you? You know why. You've already answered this question twice during the last two months."

"Would they do the same if I was the citizen of any western country?"

"You are here. Stop asking why."

"What now?"

"You know that too. No other place to go but Syria. You know that already. Stop wasting your time, get a ticket and go face your destiny."

"No! It's not the only solution. There is another one, and I still have the strength for one last battle."

"What do you mean?"

"The god of the winds, and he who said no in the face of those who said yes."

We were interrupted by the sound of the moving walkway starting up behind me, announcing the arrival of another flight.

All those months in jails, police stations and detention centres in the UAE, I never saw a white face or heard an English voice in any of the cells. Had none of them violated the labour or immigration law? Or overstayed their visa? The only time I met a westerner was at a police station one night, as I was waiting to be transferred.

The cell was full, but the door was open, to allow for more people to be shoved in. A group of men arrived, coming directly from the airport, and among them was a tall English gentleman with a white beard wearing a good suit. He stood outside the door, refusing to enter the cell.

"This is not acceptable! Don't you know who I am? How dare you bring me here? I want to call my embassy now."

He shouted and argued and demanded to call his embassy. The officers eventually told him he'd get his call if he'd just wait in the cell. We found out his crime was a financial one, like ours. He'd written a bad cheque to pay his rent, but he signed a pledge to pay the debt, so around 3:00 a.m. the man with the white beard was set free and the rest of us were transferred to our destinations with cuffs on our hands and chains on our feet. If I met any of my former cellmates now, I would have only one thing to say to them, "The system is not only broken, my friends, it's racist, too."

> Kontar_81, April 1
> When the world is judging you just because you are Syrian, 26 days stuck at Kuala Lumpur airport and I am still waiting for someone to hear.
> #war #Syria #refugees #peace #love #royal #royalfamily #story #media #newspaper #tv #help #news #journal #un #hrw #law #death #life #human #pet #photographer #photo #writer #germany #canada #usa #england #actress #actor

> @kontar81 April 10
> Add me on Snapchat! Username: hassan.kontar3

On Day 35, April 11, I googled my name. Three results only, two of which were links to my tweets. I was disheartened, but the next day, that all changed.

I didn't know it, but in Turkey, a Syrian refugee named Iman, who was waiting for relocation to Canada, found my story on Twitter. She messaged a friend, a young Syrian journalist who was living in Ghana and working for Al Jazeera. Khulod Hadaq looked up my social media feed and posted a story about it on a Facebook group for journalists. She also sent emails and messages to some journalists she knew. The impact was immediate.

On Day 35, @BBCNewsAsia sent me a direct message via Twitter.

I talked to Heather Chen on the phone and her story, headlined "Syrian Man Stranded at Malaysia Airport," was posted online by the BBC. It ran on their social media accounts and appeared on BBC networks globally.

---

[3] I never got used to Snapchat. I tried, but it seemed like something for teenagers. After I left the airport, I forgot my password and never logged in again.

"A Syrian man says he has spent over a month stranded in the transit section of a Malaysian airport, partly as a consequence of his country's civil war.

"Hassan al-Kontar's plight emerged when he began posting videos of himself at Kuala Lumpur International Airport 2. He says he was deported from the UAE to Malaysia in 2016[4], after losing his work permit when war broke out in Syria.

"He says he is unable to enter Malaysia, and that his attempts to reach Cambodia and Ecuador were also in vain.

"The airport and Malaysia's Immigration Department did not immediately respond to journalists' requests for comment."

The Washington Post picked up the story:

"When the war in Syria started, Hassan al-Kontar knew he couldn't go back. Kontar had been working in the United Arab Emirates since 2006. He had left his home to avoid conscription in the Syrian army.

"'I am a human being, and I don't consider it right to participate in war,' he told BBC. 'I'm not a killing machine, and I don't want any part in destroying Syria.'

"He has been trapped in the transit section of Kuala Lumpur International Airport 2 for 37 days."

Kaamil Ahmed, a journalist with *The Guardian* newspaper, was on a flight over Asia when he heard the BBC News Asia story. He sent me a direct message on Twitter and asked for an interview. "I can change planes in KL and meet you at the terminal," he said. The area I was in is very difficult to find, and I had trouble explaining

---

[4] This is the journalist's error; it was in fact 2017.

it to Kaamil. In the end, we could only meet on opposite sides of the glass wall that separated me from the departure area; he took a picture of me through it to accompany the article.

"'It's not my war': the Syrian man who has spent a month living in Kuala Lumpur airport.

"Hassan al-Kontar fears arrest for refusing a military call-up and now survives on airline meals of rice and chicken.

"Talking to The Guardian from behind a glass barrier to the airport's arrival corridor, which he cannot leave, Kontar said his priority was working on getting out of the airport by sending emails to rights groups and uploading daily video diaries onto Twitter – but often ends up distracted. 'You're worried about your family [and] all these psychological pressures you have but most of the time you're trying to solve your temporary issues,' said Kontar."

When I googled my name three days later, there were 27,000 hits.

My phone rang—it was my family. The story had reached Sweida. There were a lot of tears; they did not understand what I was trying to do, and they were frightened and worried. It would take me five days to convince them that this was a problem that could be turned into a solution. It wasn't my arguments that convinced them in the end, it was all the words, attention and kindness from strangers around the world that brought them on board with my plan.

The second call was from Jehad, and he was shouting, not crying. "What were you thinking? Everybody's talking about you, gloating about your situation. It's a scandal! A scandal!"

I couldn't calm him down, so in the end I shouted back, "Do you have another solution?"

"No," he shouted back.

"Then shut up." He did. It was his worry for me that had made him so angry—he didn't want the world laughing at his friend, and was afraid of what was going to happen to me. Jehad never stopped being supportive and called when he could to check on me.

> @kontar81· Apr 21, 2018
> Its not only my personal story, it's the story of each kid, mother, father, brother and sister in Syria who just want this war to stop no matter what. It's not a political story to win or lose the "throne" . . . it just a human story where everybody deserves to live in peace.

Chapter Eight

What Is It with the Media!

WHEN I WAS a kid during the 80s and early 90s, there was only media, not social media. Every morning before I went to school my father turned on the radio to listen to the BBC news. At 7:00 a.m., while it was raining and still a little dark outside, I heard their famous news countdown music with Big Ben declaring the time at the end of it. It was part of my childhood, and although they've changed it, I still like to listen to it on YouTube, looking out of my window at the grey morning light.

BBC News helped build my understanding of what is going on in the world and opened my eyes to politics. As a child, I never imagined that one day I would be the news, not just on the BBC but on other global networks, sites and newspapers too. I used Facebook and YouTube to follow some news during my early years in the UAE and thought of them as other news platforms, but I was now learning how wrong I was. In this future, we no longer watch the news, we make it and are part of it.

I'd hoped for a response but hadn't realized the Pandora's Box my social media campaign would open. Once the story exploded, I was in control of nothing—they had me now, the media and social media, and I went from being the story maker to its theme.

> @kontar81, Apr 23, 2018
> What is it with #media! I am not a political tool or a
> scoop, it doesn't matter how I sleep, it's about human
> rights and dignity

In a way, Jehad was right—it was a scandal. In the three days after Day 35, as my story went viral throughout global media, I discovered I was dealing with two different worlds, the Arab media and the western one. Their mentality, ideology and professionalism contrasted enormously. Western media used my story to highlight the Syrian war. Some used it to attack and criticize the regime and others set me up as an example of what happens to those who leave their country. Only a few looked into the humanitarian side of it. For mainstream Arab media, every story is a political one, a tool to be employed in the political or religious conflicts in the region.

I never turned down a media request for an interview. I viewed it as the opportunity to open some eyes about the humanitarian crises we were facing, how our own Arab brothers, by closing their borders to us, were party to our disaster and the death and bloodshed. Technically, I was criticizing these countries and governments but tried not to do so too directly, as I was already gaining a lot of enemies on social media. Messages began to reach me on Twitter: coward, traitor, weak, fugitive, extremist, criminal, terrorist. My first reaction was to turn off my cellphone. This had not worked the way I'd expected and I was surprised and distressed. For a while I read and replied to them all, but then I stopped. Those people have already made up their minds, I told myself, and it's hard to fill a cup that is already full. Fighting with them is nothing but a waste of time and effort, and decision-makers won't hear me out. I knew the outcome would be more division, more accusations, more negative comments and threat messages with no actual solution. I soon realized that I needed to start tweeting in English only and follow Madame Zeina's good advice.

While I never turned down an interview, the only time I walked away from one in the middle and refused to continue was with an Arabic TV channel. It was clear to me from their first questions their goal was just to make the UAE look bad. Other reporters had at least made some effort to disguise their motive, but not this interviewer. I was being used and insulted so I walked away.

Much of the western media was no better, and with the exception of a few articles and videos, I was unhappy with the way my story was being covered. Journalists would take my first words, my last words and presto! A story. The movie *The Terminal* was usually their hook and they began calling me "The Terminal Man." It was always the same questions: Have you seen the movie? How do you eat, shower, sleep? Is your life like the movie? I'd answer to satisfy their curiosity but always told them, "It's okay. I've never heard that anyone died because he had to sleep in a chair." And then I would tell them about what really mattered—the reasons why I was there in the first place.

I would tell them it was a humanitarian story, not a political one. From the beginning of my social media campaign, I had consistently stressed that this was the story of the Syrian people from 2011 onwards, suffering racism all around the world. Journalists were trying to make me a novelty interest story. The essential heart of my message—that I was refused the right to board that Turkish Airlines flight not because I was Hassan, but because I was a Syrian—disappeared from much of the coverage.

Major newspapers and TV channels didn't even contact me directly, just copied and pasted from other media. Some reporters would call once, cover the story and move on. Others, a few, would follow up and keep updating my story. Those reporters are the real deal, the ones who believe in and love what they are doing. Most of them became friends, and even now that I am safe they still check in socially.

Like Arab media, some of the western journalists also tried to use me to serve a political agenda. One famous news channel called me because they were writing an article for their website about President Trump's threats to attack Syria. First I clarified that my story was a humanitarian case and I was not involved in politics, then I added, "War is not the solution or the answer. They have been at it for a long time and it has made things worse—more people are going to suffer because of such attacks, not the regime. If Mr. Trump did such a thing, he would coordinate with Russia first. It's just a show," I told her. The next day when I visited their website, I saw the headline: "The Syrian man stuck at the airport supports Trump's attacks on Syria."

The line distinguishing humanitarian from political issues is a thin one, and sometimes it's impossible to separate the two. On occasion, I found myself forced to speak politically to give the best answer to the questions I was being asked.

During one interview with CNN, the host asked me: "Why can't you come to the USA?"

"Because as a Syrian, I am subject to the travel ban. We can't enter the USA, not for work, tourism, study, investment or even if we are married to an American citizen but don't have a green card."

"Oh, yes, the Trump ban. What do you think about it?"

"I just can't understand how someone, anyone, can be against his own roots. Here we have a man, his father was an immigrant, his mother was an immigrant, two of his wives are immigrants, which makes him and his sons, sons of immigrants. Yet he does all he can to deny us the same rights his parents, wives and kids have. It's not the Syrian people who are launching terror attacks on US soil, but in Syria we have 850 American citizens fighting with the extremists. It's not Syria who has troops inside US borders, it's America who has eight military bases in our land." They edited the interview and cut this, keeping the story more casual—more Tom Hanks than Hassan.

One media incident in particular made me feel betrayed and angry. Because of the media coverage, I began receiving messages from other refugees, from all over the world. One was from a man living in Nauru Island in Oceania, northeast of Papua New Guinea. The Australian government sent refugees there, hundreds of them, after denying their right to seek asylum, without even a trial. This man started sending me photos and videos about the situation there—inhuman was not a strong enough word to describe it, but the only one I could think of. He begged me to speak out about them and I felt a responsibility to do so. I promised him I would try.

"The Project," a TV show on the Australian Network 10 channel, contacted me, asking me for an interview. Great, I thought, this is my chance to speak out about the situation, to keep my promise and to educate the Australian people about what was going on. I believed it was a live show—that even if they tried to interrupt me or change the subject, I'd find a way to deliver my message—but I was wrong. That's when I learned that they build in a fifteen-minute delay. People think it's live but it's not, and the delay gives them time to edit and control the show.

Their first question was, "How is the duty-free?" They kept asking similar questions about my daily life and at the very end, they asked if there was anything else I wanted to say. That was my cue.

"Yes, I do. I have a message for the Australian government. You can't, as a part of the international community, abuse people just to make them an example. You can't ignore your obligations towards international law, you can't disrespect your own signature. Australia is a signatory of the 1951 Refugee Convention since 1954, yet you are locking people away for years, with no trial, no medical care, no electricity, nothing. If the Australian government lost its copy of the convention somewhere, I will be happy to send them mine."

They made no comment but thanked me for being with them and wished me luck. I felt happy, proud. I felt that I achieved something, that I'd spoke out to correct things. Then they posted the program on social media and I had my wake-up call. They had edited my comments out. It broke me how I'd let that man and those people down, that they believed I hadn't tried, and that I'd not kept my promise. Some media made me feel like a phoenix, rising from the ashes, providing their platform for the world to listen. Others, like Network 10, showed me I was just a comic Don Quixote fighting windmills.

It was just another normal morning day, about Day 39 or 40, and I was watching the airplanes, listening to the flight announcements and still not understanding what she was saying, checking my phone now and then for updates. I noticed some unusual activity on my Twitter account, the kind of spike that normally came after a new media story about me had been published. There wasn't supposed to be anything today, I said to myself. What is going on? Then I saw that Jamal Khashoggi was following me and had retweeted one of my tweets. The rest of the world would learn about him after he was assassinated and brutally cut up into pieces, but for those of us in the Arab world he was a well-known, if controversial, character.

He used to work as a consultant for one of the Saudi princes and was a powerful man with a lot of authority and a luxurious life. But then he decided to start saying NO in his own way, using his pen to tell the truth as a journalist working for *The Washington Post*. He wasn't as powerful as he had been, but he was still an influencer, with many followers. I had not tagged him or reached out to him, but he'd come to me. I sent him a message, thanking him for his kindness, and for being the voice for those who had none. He replied the next day with a short message wishing me all the best. Minutes later a second message arrived:

> Hassan, your last message was wonderful, in which you
> combined your personal suffering with that of millions

of Arab youth. I suggest that you always add with every
message you post and after you talk a little bit about
yourself and the developments of your situation, to add a
word about the cause that made you end up at the airport, tell us about revolution, hope for freedom, the Arab
Spring, justices, employment, tell us about a generation
that lacks education. Tell us why we need peace in the
Arab world!
I am trying to help you with an American friend here but
now I can't promise anything, hold on, every day your
lovers and those who pray for you increase.

I replied, "I will keep your words in my mind, and will always work
according to them. Humanity is my cause. Thank you, sir, for your
support."

Khashoggi did not lie to me and he didn't make any promises. He
did what he could, but we both knew that is almost impossible for a
Syrian to travel to the USA because of the travel ban.

In one of his early press conferences about me, the Malaysian
Minister of Home Affairs said, "We need to do a security check on
him. What if he is a terrorist or belongs to ISIS?" From my chair
at the airport, with my phone in my hand, I was dealing with the
first media storm and wondering how to handle it. They wanted to
demonize me, but at least they'd acknowledged that I existed. As I
read his words online, I thought, "This can't be a government minister! He has the resources and employees to find out about me. He
is using it as a ploy, just to deal with the media. Should I post something about it? Should I tell him that it's ideologically impossible, as
I belong to a minority?" That night, when some investigators paid
me their usual visit, I told them, "Use Google. It will not take long
for your Minister to find out if I belong to ISIS or not. Just google
my name, the city where I'm from and you will know. You don't
need a whole intelligence service to do that! Just a laptop or phone."

The minority card was one that I had refused to play since Day 1 at the airport. The issue of rights for ethnic, racial, and religious minorities is a sensitive one, especially in the west, and early in the war the Syrian regime used this to market itself to the international community. The government argued that it was the protector of minorities, especially Christians. To make this pressure tactic more effective, Bashar al-Assad withdrew his forces from minority areas to allow ISIS to attack, just to remind the world that he was the protector. This happened in Sweida and Maaloula, Druze and Christian areas respectively, and I swore never to represent myself as Druze, but as a human being and a Syrian. How could I address the world about my basic rights as a human and about the new type of racism all Syrians were facing, while playing the role of a persecuted minority trying to save myself? If someone asked me about my religious background, I did not refuse to answer, but I never mentioned it first, nor did I start with it. I wasn't going to give the Syrian regime any opportunity to use me as one of their playing cards.

While no one from Arab media visited me at the airport, the western media did, ignoring my warnings about how risky it was. They didn't listen and just kept showing up. "Fine, if you want to do so, I can't stop you," I'd say to them, "but please act like a passenger who just knows who I am and who's come to say hi. Don't show any mics, cameras, or even a notebook. They are watching and they will come to join us, sit near us, just to check what is going on." That was my request, and it went well with newspaper journalists most of the time, but with TV crews, holding their big cameras and lights, it was another story that would cause all of us some problems.

The first TV crew to visit me at the airport was from HBO's "Vice News Tonight" and consisted of the host, Hind Hassan (a UK citizen originally from Iraq), Lorial the producer, cameraman Daniel and their Malaysian "fixer" Joshua. The interviews I was giving were provoking the local authorities and putting me at risk, but it was a risk I needed to take. However, a TV crew showing up at the airport was a new whole level of provocation and, as I expected, the officials came running. They had three main worries. The first was that their general election was coming up and they didn't want any negative publicity about their country. The second issue was that they'd recently received significant international criticism from human rights organizations and media over the case of two gay women who'd been arrested for kissing in a parking area and would be sentenced to a public caning under Sharia law. The third was that the international coverage I was getting made me another black mark on their human rights record and also an embarrassment.

The media stories that mentioned my criticism of the Air Asia food I was being given made them particularly upset and angry. The authorities, and a lot of Malaysian people, took it personally, accusing me of making fun of their country and culture. I received thousands of inappropriate messages and comments. While I could understand that they thought their country was being attacked and they wanted to defend it, what they didn't understand was that I was just talking about my daily life at the airport. If I'd been eating the most delicious dish from the finest Parisian restaurant three times a day for months, I would get sick of it too.

The airport authorities and officials had no experience with how to deal with a TV crew, and Joshua the Malaysian fixer kept them occupied while the Vice News Tonight crew recorded the video, taking about two hours to complete the interview and shoot. The NBC America crew who came later weren't so lucky. Agents from a number of departments came, separated us, and forced the crew to erase all videos after interrogating them for hours.

Visits from the police and immigration officials increased. Now that I was the focus of media attention, the interrogations weren't after midnight in the corridor. Now it was higher-ranking officials inviting me for "meetings" in their office, where they'd offer me tea with milk. Whenever they questioned me there were different teams, different faces, different departments, different times, but there was always something in common. The room became smaller, the air too heavy to breathe, and time moved more slowly. What amused me was how confused they were and how stupid some of them could be. I don't think it's just Malaysia, it's worldwide. It's the way they are trained to be: ignorant, always suspicious, only concerned with one thing, to intimidate you into admitting their "truth."

Speaking to three high-ranking immigration officers at the airport during one of their many, many long interrogations, I said, "Do you want me to say something good to the media about Malaysia?"

"No."

"Something bad then?"

"No, no. No one likes bad publicity."

"What about something good? Why don't you want it?"

"We don't want people to follow in your footsteps and start show-ing up at our airport."

"You don't want me to say something good or bad. What is it that you want exactly?"

"We don't know."

"It's going to happen anyway."

"What?"

"People will follow in my footsteps, but make no mistake. Not because they are inspired by me but because of the system."

"What about the system?"

"The system is broken, sir, and if I were you, I would make myself ready. They are coming anyway."

And they did. When I met my two Egyptian friends that first night at the airport, I hadn't known how many more I would meet: twenty-six to be exact.[5] They all had the same problem, denied entry to Korea and being deported back to Egypt through Malaysia. Most

---

[5] I would also meet and help thirty-two Yemenis, three Sudanese, four from Somalia and two Syrians. One of them was returning to Syria; the other was waiting for his study visa to Malaysia.

of them would stay for about a week. With time, the staff began sending every man who got stuck to me, so I could guide them through what to do. I was the expert. I became like a comfort zone for them, and they would follow me everywhere and join me under the escalator to sleep. They were scared, and it was my turn to tell them that everything was going to be okay.

Since I arrived in Canada, because I am known as the "guy from the airport," people who get stuck at airports still message me, asking for help (thirteen of them so far, half of them in Kuala Lumpur Airport). Whenever I receive such messages, I remember the faces of those three high-ranking immigration officers, together in that cold room full of desks, drinking their tea with milk, trying to hide their true faces and playing nice. I wonder if they think about what I told them: "The system is broken, and they will keep coming."

As weeks progressed, officials began a campaign to make my life more difficult. I used to spend most of my time sitting on the metal seats distributed along the corridors, looking through the glass wall to the runway outside. It was quieter there and perfect for media interviews, but then the staff decided to move all the seating from the corridor to the waiting hall, in front of the customer service office. They wanted to keep me in their sight, so they could limit and monitor any personal meetings or interviews.

Since the customer service office dealt with transit passengers who needed to change their ticket or who had a problem, the area always had people who were forced to wait. Some of them began to join me at my sleeping area under the escalator, and this annoyed the officials even further. They would come frequently to kick me out, removing the yellow barriers I'd put up for privacy. Each night, I'd sneak back and set it all up again.

What I was learning about how traditional news media worked taught me more about social media—how to understand and how to use it. When you run your social media account, you own it: no one can cut or edit it, you can correct false information, you can present your point of view. Social media would be my tool to balance the media coverage that was being generated about me.

Drawing the attention of YouTube, Instagram, Facebook and Twitter influencers helped my social media campaign. Christina Galbato, the blogger and online educator, heard my story and decided to speak out. Sharing and letting her hundreds of thousands of followers know was her way of helping, a powerful one. People would come up to me at the airport saying, "We heard about you from Christina."

Lakshmi Priyaa Chandramouli (39,000 Instagram followers), the Indian actor, was another active supporter, as was the French entrepreneur, humanitarian and Snapchat celebrity Jérôme Jarre (1.3 million followers on Twitter). They were creating a wave, these influencers—along with the likes of Facebook pages such as Brut, LADbible and UNILAD—a wave to pressure the powerful to help my case. They were also building a shield to prevent the Malaysian government and airport authorities from harming me. I realized quickly that these influencers were formulating public opinion, crossing borders and nationalities. People don't need to carry a sign or join a protest march, they can lead change from their room, with their phone or laptop. They are the future of political change and hashtags are their language.

Before the airport, I'd thought about social media platforms as places where rumours flourished and anger flowed. A place where people could hide behind fake names and profile photos, some to spread hate and racism, others to gather likes, fame and money. As I was learning, it could be a hostile environment, because many good people who saw posts and tweets and cared did not engage with me directly, while those who didn't like what I was saying filled my feed with hate-filled comments. Now I saw Twitter, Facebook and Instagram were just tools—ones that could be used for greater good or greater evil, weapons of mass distraction or mass destruction. Those negative, accusatory comments were overwhelmed by the messages of love and a thousand prayers from all over the world. Whenever I was feeling lonely and weak, under the escalator or walking the corridors, I would open messages from people I'd never met, who were my saviours, my army and my source of power.

Chapter Nine

Heroes

ON APRIL 27 (Day 50), I recorded another video:

> Hello, Guys. I have some important news. And this time
> it is serious, it's not about coffee and some jokes. When
> the rest of the world was watching, or ignoring or making
> me their scoop, a great country, a really humanitarian
> society, decided to stand up and show other govern-
> ments how to behave. Canada is what I am speaking
> about. An amazing group of volunteers have been wor-
> king behind the scenes . . .

> @kontar18 Apr 27, 2018
> Plz retweet I have Some good news and I need your help
> all of you to make it happen. Please send an email to
> Mr. Ahmed Hussen - Canada's Minister of Immigration.
> "ahmed.hussen@parl.gc.ca" Tell him you support a
> Temporary Resident Permit for Hassan to come to
> Canada immediately.

Iman, the Syrian woman living in Turkey who sent the message to
Khulod in Ghana, had introduced me and my story to a woman
named Vanja at the same time. Vanja was an immigrant from the

former Yugoslavia, who'd been living in Canada for years and was involved with a humanitarian group there that sponsored and helped refugees. Vanja shared my story with two people: Laurie Cooper in Whistler, BC, and Stephen Watt in Toronto, Ontario. They both sent me friend requests on Facebook and connected on WhatsApp.

I did not pay much attention in the beginning. People were reaching out to me all the time, advising me what to do or whom to contact. "I know the wife of Sultan of Boronia and she owes me a favour, he also has a private jet he can send to you, what do you think?" "I know some parliament members in this country, some minsters, and senators, what do you think?" I never turned any of them down—I knew they wanted to help—but they didn't understand the system. I'd thank them and say, let us try. I didn't tell them what I knew—this was not how the real world worked. Personal connections are useful to speed up the process, but officials and even politicians are employees who will always cover themselves first and take no risks with the law and their careers.

Stephen Watt and Laurie Cooper were different. Stephen was in his forties but looked younger. He is a marketing manager at the University of Toronto, who became involved in the refugee crisis when he received a blog post in 2016 from a neighbour, asking for volunteers to help the 35,000 Syrian refugees who were coming to Canada. He's a master at connecting people. He isn't part of any official organization, but he knows most of them, and we called him our super-connector. He writes the story of individual refugees, sends it to his network and helps them figure out the sponsorship application, without directly sponsoring them himself.

Laurie, a former CBC producer, was then in her mid-fifties. She'd been aiding refugees at camps in Greece since 2015, volunteering at Lesbos twice, and had set up a group of volunteers called Canada Caring to help refugees come to Canada, successfully helping twelve. I wasn't her first case, but I would turn out to be her most challenging as mine was not a "normal" refugee case. People say hope is the light at the end of the tunnel but for me, hope had a human face—Laurie's. Laurie was the leader of the team I call my Avengers.

Stephen and Laurie communicated via emails and WhatsApp, asking me questions about my life and what happened to me. They wanted to authenticate my story and confirm that I was telling the truth and not hiding anything. Then Laurie arranged to get a new cellphone to me, a genuine Samsung, through a Canadian teacher working in Malaysia. Up until then, I'd been using my fake, Chinese-made Samsung and this precious tool that connected me to the outside was a moody one, turning on and off whenever it wanted to. I wouldn't be able to breathe until it started up again, terrified that it might shut down permanently. Now I could relax.

In one of our first WhatsApp conversations, Stephen asked me: "Do you have any thoughts about living in Canada, by the way?"

"It's Canada . . . CANADA. I think you got my answer with the capital letters." Canada was way beyond my wildest dreams. It was too good to be true, and I didn't believe anything would come of this.

But then they both came back with a plan, a real plan, and I needed to start paying attention. Laurie said that it would be easier to get me into Canada if I were in Ecuador, and she was contacting the Ecuadorean government about a visa and airlines about flights. I didn't stop her, but I knew it wasn't going to work, as I'd tried that already, but she needed to try herself so she would believe me. Sponsorship for Canadian residency was the only solution, and that was the answer that she and Stephen came up with.

Laurie didn't contact me a lot, just quick chats to check on me to see if I needed anything or to update me about what was going on. She was working on it, I knew, and that was more than enough. Even though I was desperate, I tried to give her space and not pressure her. Laurie is working on it, I told myself. She believes in me and there is no need to pester her.

After hearing an interview with Laurie and me on CBC Radio's "As It Happens," a Canadian lawyer called the CBC to get Laurie's contact details. Andrew Brouwer offered her his help, not asking for a single dollar. Some people were saying I was turning down offers of help, but the truth was simpler—although I'd been in the news all over the world, sometimes in languages I didn't even know existed, Andrew was the only lawyer in the world who heard my story and stepped forward to offer real help. He arranged to get all the documents I needed to sign to me at KLIA2 via a passenger, an American teacher working in Kuala Lumpur.

> @kontar81 May 8, 2018
> I keep reading the reviews regarding the new #avengers. FYI I am more luckier than most of you as I have my own real avengers team they are making the world a better place to live. They believe in humanity no matter what. @ canadacaring I love you guys and I owe you everything

In one of my posts, I asked if anyone knew Iron Man's number, as I wanted to rent his suit to fly out of the airport. It sounded funny the way I spoke about it, and I wanted people to laugh, but for me it was more than a joke. I now had my own Avenger team.

Sitting on a chair at the airport, my phone in my hand, I was receiving messages from people all around the world. "You are a hero, you are an inspiration." Their intentions were good. They wanted to encourage me and make me feel better, but their words weighed heavily on me. What makes us heroes? Asking for your basic human rights is not a heroic act. It's what we should all do. I thought a lot about it and still do. The System convinces us that it offers our rights, and we should take them and be grateful. If you challenge, if you say no and ask for more rights as a human being, if you make your issue not a personal one but a greater one, then you may become a hero in the eyes of others—those who believe in the same thing but do nothing—whether you want to or not. Like Marvel Comics characters, one hero can't get the job done, he'll get his ass kicked. Heroes need help from other heroes and that was exactly what was happening with me. My Avengers were Laurie, Stephen and Mr. Andrew, as I called him. They weren't tough and aggressive, but kind, soft, humble and determined. They were hope.

Stephen visited me in May at KLIA2, modifying a trip to Asia he planned earlier to layover for two days in Malaysia. "You look shorter in real life," were his first words to me. Then he handed me a bag with some things I'd asked for: a battery bank, phone charger and a headset. During the seven months I spent at the airport, I lost eight phone chargers and five battery banks. Someone was taking them, and it was driving me crazy. I never found out who it was but felt it couldn't be a coincidence. All my complaints to the airport authorities received the same answer: "Sorry. The security camera wasn't pointing at where you were sitting." Strangely, every time I was seated in a different place, and every time the camera was pointing in the opposite direction. They were monitoring me 24/7, and this was another of their ways to make my life difficult. Perhaps they thought that their problem wasn't with me but with my cellphone. It was the enemy, and they would do whatever they could to shut it down.

The day before Stephen left, we spent four hours chatting, laughing and giving each other comfort. He gave me a bottle of whisky. It didn't take long for Krishna to discover it and when I was away from my spot, he filled his water bottle with it and got drunk at work. The other last gift from Stephen on that visit was the photo he took of me, in front of the huge world map that hung on the wall in one of the corridors. He posted it on social media, with the caption "Big unwelcoming world." It became the most famous photo of me at the airport.

A message came from Laurie: "The BC Muslim Association is

going to sponsor you." I could tell how happy she was, but at the time, I didn't fully understand what this meant, or why it would be so important. "Cool," I messaged back. It turned out to be very important indeed. The BCMA heard my story and they reached out to Laurie, offering their help. As simple as that, just another case and another sponsorship, as they were doing all the time. One member in particular, Shawkat Hasan, played a key part behind the scenes, never speaking to me or contacting me directly. He and others from the Association were there to greet me at Vancouver International Airport, and they never once asked for any kind of credit or media coverage. And it didn't matter to them that I was Druze.

I was receiving thousands of messages daily on all my social media accounts, and I don't remember why this one person stood out and how we started texting and talking each day. I've asked him, and he doesn't remember either. What I know is that he is my brother from another mother. Trust has to be built over time, with effort from both sides and tested with real problems and situations. It needs personal, face-to-face meetings, where eyes can connect and read the unspoken words. Dr. Osama and I have never met, but I trust this hero like I trust no other person.

Dr. Osama is a Sudanese man with a PhD in mechanical engineering who has been living and working in Malaysia for years. Someone sent him an article in Arabic that was critical of me, knowing that Dr. Osama was someone who had a history of defending vulnerable people and helping refugees in Malaysia. He'd been born and raised in a corrupt dictatorial regime himself, so he knew what it felt like to be exiled, oppressed and powerless. He was well-educated and cultured, and informed about the refugee crisis, having worked with NGOs in the past. However it started, having calls and messages from Dr. Osama made my life easier. He was there day and night. Whenever I called, he would answer; whatever

I needed, he would find a way to get to me. If I was going through a hard time (my phone charger stolen again) and feeling low, I would call him. When I was happy and optimistic I would call him too. He used Krishna's bank account to send me money, even though I hadn't asked. "Just keep it with you," he used to say, "In case you need something or something urgent comes up." He never asked for his money back.

@kontar81, June 3
TIME TO LEAVE. Human right, international law, organizations, governments, media, they all could not or dont want to help. Maybe it's time to try science.

To: NASA
Subject: Job application
Dear NASA:
My name is Hassan, I am from Syria, 36 years old, SINGLE, currently living at Kuala Lumpur international airport since 87 days, and I would like to apply/volunteer for your next expedition to Mars.
Please note that I have so many strength points and the perfect reasons to dedicate myself to such mission:
It's very clear by now that there is no place for me on this earth as no country is allowing me in.
I have a lot of space movies experience so I know my way around a spaceship including space combat from star war movies so it will not take long time for you to train me.
I am a small size man so no need for a big ship, a small one will do with second hand equipment made in China which will reduce your expenses.
If anything gone wrong please send no rescue mission as I had enough from this big unwelcoming world.
It's completely FREE OF CHARGE.

> I will pay for my medical exam and training lessons and
> my light saber space sword if I need any.
> Waiting your kind and URGENT reply.
> Thanks and regards,
> Hassan KLIA2

Laurie and the Avengers at Canada Caring had done so much for me: they'd found me a sponsor, a job at a hotel (even though this was not a requirement) and they'd submitted my application to come to Canada as a refugee.

Laurie called me to let me know I had my "G" number and that I was officially in the system. The normal processing time is about twenty-four months from the date of application. "If it is just a matter of time, if that is all that it is, I can wait," I told her. "I will wait for twenty-four months."

There were petitions and campaigns, and the publicity in international media generated even more social media pressure to get the Canadian government to speed up the process. People from around the world were sending emails to the Minister and Prime Minister, asking them to expedite my application.

> @canadacaring Jul 12, 2018
> Say "happy birthday" to Hassan today by asking
> Canada's Prime Minister @JustinTrudeau to help him
> get to Canada after 4 months in the KL Airport. Please
> retweet! @kontar81 @cafreeland @HonAhmedHussen
> @JennyKwanBC @pgoldsmithjones @CBCNews @
> CTVNews @globeandmail @guardian @amnesty

Some might say they were ignoring this media pressure, but I saw it differently, both then and now. It was about priorities. How could a young, single guy—who was living with a roof above his head, had three meals a day (even if they were all the same meal), a phone and the internet, coffee and toilets—be more of a priority than a family with children, perhaps one of them ill, living in a tent in a refugee camp? If I were a Canadian immigration official, I'd choose the family in the blink of an eye.

The Canadian government was monitoring my situation and following my news, but they had an obligation to the Canadian people to study my application, check out me and my story, and they had the right to do so. And that took time, as well I knew. Later, when I was arrested and in real danger, then I became a priority.

My story was viral, and as it grew, so the rank of the officials coming to meet me at the airport rose. The CEO of the Malaysian NGO, Malaysian Humanitarian Aid and Relief (MAHAR), visited me at the airport with a proposal. MAHAR had been set up in 2017 but is not recognized by the UNHCR or international law. It offers refugees a temporary card to stay in the country when their visa expires, but it can be withdrawn at any time and holders have no right to work, education or healthcare. If they caught you working with a MAHAR card, that meant arrest and deportation. MAHAR's establishment was a political move, to say to the world that Malaysia was doing something for refugees when in reality it was not.

The CEO tried to convince me to leave the airport and apply for a MAHAR card.

"Will you give me a card before I leave the airport?" I asked.

"No. You must leave, then complete the application," he said.

There were rumours that Druze minority people were not being accepted for the program. Either way, I did not trust them. Clearly, they just wanted to get me out of the airport, to reduce the international attention I was getting. Who would remember me after two months if I accepted such an offer? What would happen to me when my passport expired again? It would only be a matter of time before I was illegal again in Malaysia and I would have to relive what I'd gone through for years in the UAE. No, I said. No more temporary solutions.

Later, he called me to offer a six-month visa. I asked him if I could stay for twenty-four months, as that was how long it was going to take for the Canadian application to be approved, but he refused. Only six months, he said.

"What am I going to do Day One after the six months end and my Canadian application is not yet approved?" He didn't answer and ended the call. I knew that they just wanted me to stop being in the media, to stop damaging and embarrassing them in the eyes of the world.

The UNHCR in Malaysia, who'd ignored the emails I'd sent and responded to a phone call with a we-can't-do-anything reply, also paid me a visit now that I was an international story. They were under pressure too, their reputation coming under scrutiny from both social and traditional media. They interviewed me, promised to issue me a UNHCR card. However, rather than helping, they worked to damage my reputation. One of their spokespeople claimed that I was a "country shopper" who had turned down offers from other countries even though they knew that the only country who had offered me a solution was Canada. The Malaysian government was using them.

When you spend so much time in the same place and become familiar with all its features—the exits, lights, signs and endless dong-dong-dongs and announcements from its speakers—you know that parts of it are mocking you. But you chose to ignore it and make your peace with them: the big map on the wall of the world with no place in it for me; the flight departures screen but not one is yours; the slogan on the side of the planes ("Air Asia, where everyone can fly"); the lights that burn twenty-four hours a day. When there is a change in this familiar environment, it can take a moment to understand it. I was just walking around on Day 122 when I smelled something strange and felt something weird touch my face. I spun around to see that one of the cleaning staff had opened the door to the outside to clean the stairs. The strange smell was fresh air, hot and wet but fresh. For two whole minutes, the time it took her to finish and close the door, I stood there enjoying it.

One night, I was walking to get some hot water for my coffee, and something was strange, not right. Some of the corridor lights were not working—a partial electricity failure—and it was *dark*. Whenever I wanted to sleep, I had to pull a hood over my head and cover my face, so I could have some darkness. It was suffocating, and I never got used to it. On both these occasions I took photos to memorialize them, and as a reminder that the way I was living was *not* normal.

Chapter Ten

You're a Celebrity Now

"YOU ARE A celebrity now" is what police, officials and airport staff would say to me. I didn't contradict them, because if they believed that, it was a kind of protection. It worked for a while, until they felt they couldn't handle or control it any longer, and decided to try to end it.

The truth is that I never felt like a celebrity, more like a zoo animal. Celebrities have their own jets, they don't get stuck at airports. One day, I was sitting on the floor, charging my phone, leaning against the wall, when I noticed a lady pointing her phone at me from a distance, taking photos. She didn't come up to say hi or ask how I was doing. She took her photos, smiled and walked away.

A passenger came up to me. "I have a lawyer in the city, he is going to help you. I need to take a selfie with you so I can show him."

"Hell of a lawyer you have," I replied. He took his photo and left.

One time I was seated on my spot when a lady approached. I could not see her face properly, because it was blocked by her camera attached to a stick. I saw the red light showing that she was recording.

"Are you recording me?" I asked.

"Yes, but I just came to say hi." I asked her to turn it off. She did and left.

Another lady sent me a message, asking for what she called a favour. "I need to take a selfie with you."

"Is that the favour you want? Sure, I will be glad to."

"The thing is that I made a bet with a friend. He is going to give me €500 if I get a selfie with you. I am going to use the money to save pets."

I did not refuse—I love pets too—but it seemed to me that people lose perspective sometimes. I just answered, "Sure. But what about me? Who is going to save me?"

She never turned up, and I never heard from her again.

I learned to study the people I met, to understand their type first so I knew how to deal with them. Look them up and down, then ask a question or two to evaluate their personality. Are they the serious type? Funny? Smart? Stupid? Are they a caring person or not? Are they after a photo to post or a hug to make me feel better? Are they going to ask me "Have you seen *The Terminal*?" or are they going to ask how I'm doing and what I need? I met them all and dealt with them all, but it wasn't as if I had a choice to ignore those who did not actually care. They knew how to find me, they were the visitors who bought a ticket to enter the zoo, and I was the monkey in the cage waiting for them to take a photo, throw a banana and leave.

Some of the people who contacted me weren't interested in a humanitarian cause. I think they'd never given it a thought, and all they saw was an opportunity to exploit me, a wave they could ride and take advantage of. If I'd paid any attention to this group of people while I was at the airport, I would have made a small fortune.

"Man! Let us do it."

"Do what exactly?"

"Do some business. I manufacture sports shoes. I will send you some shoes I've designed and you will start wearing and advertising them. I will give you ten percent of each sale."

"Great! And I will make sure the police agents wear them too, as they keep kicking me out from where I sleep. It will be a great advertisement. You want me to advertise your shoes while I am at the airport trying to tell the world who we really are as Syrians? If I did such a thing I would be telling them that we are nothing but greedy people who take every opportunity to make money. Sir, thank you but I am telling the story and not selling it."

A lady who owned a catering company sent me a direct message on Twitter: "Give me your mail address, I will send you all the food you want. We should speak about it more."

I didn't respond. I checked her Twitter account and didn't have a good feeling about her. By now, I was getting good at telling from the messages I received who really cared and who seemed suspicious. I'd wait for her to show her real face and what she was really after. Two days later she sent me another message: "How dare you ignore my message when I was trying to feed you! I hope you remain there forever and burn in Hell. You deserve it."

A documentary director approached me with the suggestion that I shoot my own movie. He sent me an Amazon link to the kind of mics and camera I should buy. "I will give you 10% of the revenue, but you must sign an exclusive contract with me."

"Thank you," I replied, "but no." He kept sending me messages for a while, but I didn't respond again.

They say the cynical man is an idealistic man who feels disappointed. I choose to respond to rude people with a joke or irony. I wouldn't let them get under my skin or ruin my day more than it already had been.

A European woman woke me up at around 3:00 a.m., during the precious few hours I could sleep at night, from 1:30 until 4:00. I woke up with a sense of resentment and reached out my hand to search for my glasses. I expected to see familiar faces, the police and investigators who visited and woke me up at this time, but I was wrong. The second I put on my glasses and saw her pale face, I saw her confident, entitled look.

"Yes, how can I help you?"

"Are you the man who lives here?"

"Live here! It's more stuck here, but go on, please."

"Where did you bring your mattress from? My flight has been delayed by seven hours and I need to sleep."

"Did you just wake me up to ask me about my mattress? Are you serious?" My camping mattress was a gift from one of the teachers.

"Yes, I need to buy one, then you can have it."

"You don't buy a mattress, you own it. You need to spend at least fifty days sleeping on a floor or a chair. Then you can have one."

"I don't understand."

"I don't expect you to."

"What about yours? Would you want to sell it, or rent it? You can keep the money and I will give it back to you in the morning. It's seven hours! What I am going to do?"

"How tired are you? Listen, I used to work as a magician. I would love you to leave now before I make you disappear."

During one of the many mornings I spent sitting on the floor with my coffee, charging my phone and staying around to make sure no one stole the charger—again—an American woman, very beautiful, approached me.

"Hi, I know who you are and I have a question for you, please."

"Hi, sure."

"You've been sitting here for a long time, and I thought it's a good idea to ask you. Have you noticed any passengers travelling with their pets? I have a cat and I love it so much and I need to know what to do so they will allow her to travel with me."

"I am so sorry, I never paid any attention to be honest. I am more focused on finding a way to travel myself first. Being at the airport for a long time doesn't make me an aviation consultant.

I can show you the customer service office. You can check with them."

If there were devils, there were angels too. A group of eight teachers working in Kuala Lumpur, from Canada and the US, decided to help, motivated by their humanity. All eight came looking for me the first time they visited, on their way back from a weekend in Thailand. They brought a suitcase full of clothes, hygiene products, food and basic medicines. After they left, I discovered the money they'd hidden inside. They began to visit me regularly, individually, loaded with whatever they thought I might need. It was normal for me to wake up or to come back to my spot to find a bag they left with a note. They made sure not to wake me if I was sleeping, as they knew how much I needed it and how rare it was, so they would just leave the bag, always with a coffee balanced on top. Sometimes I would message them and tell them things were okay, there was nothing I needed, but it made no difference, they'd bring something anyway. It helped a lot.

A Canadian family, originally from Vancouver but now living and working in Indonesia, visited me twice. The first time, I came back to my spot to find a full suitcase. I didn't look inside, thinking it belonged to a transit passenger who'd left it there and would be back soon. Hours passed before I realized it was for me. When I opened it, it was full of instant coffee. An American couple from Hawaii, a Portuguese family, an Australian who insisted on spending half a day with me to cheer me up. People would visit and bring me stuff, including Mediterranean food, thinking I would be missing it. I can't mention them all, or this book would be too heavy to carry.

I'd written a post about *The Terminal* movie, and how Tom Hanks had Catherine and I had no one. "Bring me Catherine and I will stay here for as long as she wants." A comment from a Canadian woman arrived—"I could be your Catherine Zeta-Jones"—and she began sending me short, sincere messages. Reading what people sent helped to pass the time, and it made me smile to feel the love from these individuals. There was nothing they could do but offer me words, but those kind words helped me keep my faith in humanity. The Canadian "Catherine" told me she wanted to help but didn't know how or what to do. "I could marry you," she offered. Hers was the first, but not the last, marriage proposal I received. It was also the sweetest.

Most of the proposals came from the USA. For me, that was proof that it's a land full of good people who want to help, but don't know how. Some of the American women who wrote to me had a sense of humour. "You look too cute for a man your age," one said. I replied, "You wanted to call me grandpa at the end of that message, didn't you?" Another lovely woman apologized in advance. "I'm sorry for not being romantic, but I will marry you on paper if it helps you get out of your situation."

Responding to these marriage offers made me feel shy and confused. Speaking to women is not one of my strengths, and to most of them, I said little beyond, "Thank you for trying to help."

One American lady offered what she said was my only real solution—to marry her. When I turned her down, she sent this message: "You know!! You had an opportunity that you rejected, I think you are enjoying the attention that you have never ever received in your entire life." Her precise words.

"The hell I can't marry you!! I work for a congressman, and I can marry whomever I want," another one messaged me.

"Yes," I responded, "you can marry whomever you want, it's your personal freedom, but bringing your Syrian husband to the USA is an entirely different matter. It's not about your personal freedom anymore, it is the law. I am afraid you will need to move in and live with me at the airport if you decide to proceed." That was my answer but what I was really thinking was that a woman who claims she is working for a congressman should know better than that. There was a travel ban—Syrians couldn't enter the USA, not as students, tourists, workers, investors, or spouses. Stupid, I know, but the truth.

I politely explained this in response to each American who proposed to me. I added that, even if there was no travel ban, the law sees it as fraud, and it's illegal to marry someone just to get them into the country. I did not reject their offers because I didn't want to be married, I rejected them because it was the wrong solution and it would have caused both of us legal problems. All I was asking for was legal permanent status. And I simply could not trade love for safety.

My potential love life was broadcast to the world after a reporter from Vice.com came to see me. Nyima Pratten was heavily armed with gifts, including the most precious one—coffee. Her gift meant that for the whole week I didn't need to worry about running out. Another of her gifts was ironic, a copy of an inflight magazine. I remember drinking the coffee and ignoring the magazine. The article she wrote went viral, especially in the Arab world. Maybe because she cleverly chose to make the title "People are offering to marry the Syrian refugee stuck in an airport." She was correct. I did receive marriage proposals from both genders. One of the Arabic comments about me on the Vice feature said, "He is 100% naturally stupid."

One of my two Egyptian friends from the first days at the airport had met a Japanese lady the day I landed. He spoke no English and she spoke no Arabic, but the guy saw an opportunity. He figured that if he could make her fall in love with him and marry him, he'd get to Japan. For the next three days, while he was waiting for his ticket, I acted as his translator, chatting with her on WhatsApp and writing whatever he told me to. The Egyptian guy was not a bad guy, he was a desperate one, like most Arab guys these days.

She did not take him seriously. She was laughing at him, but I didn't tell him that. I didn't want to take away his dream, and I think it helped him smile and pass the time at the airport. That is what the proposals did for me in any case, and for that I will always be grateful to those people who didn't know how the system worked but were trying to help in their own way.

While I was walking around one night, an Asia Air flight attendant came up to me. She was very beautiful, tall, black hair, from eastern Europe. I'd never seen her before, and said to myself, "My Catherine Zeta-Jones has landed and she's a hundred percent real." What came out of her mouth was one of those stupid questions with obvious answers that I hate.

"Hey, I am following your story."

"Thank you."

"So, how is life?"

"Life could not be better. Look around you."

"So, you are still here?"

"What? No, no. I just came back yesterday."

"Why?"

"I missed my chair."

My Catherine gave me an I-am-going-to-kill-you look and left. I never saw her again.

One encounter is my favourite one, and it makes me smile every time I remember it. The heroes were a married couple from Singapore, in their late twenties, polite and kind. The guy knew who I was—he read about me somewhere—but the lady, she had no idea who I was or why her husband decided to stop and say hi. They sat on either side of me, and he spoke across me to his wife.

"Honey, do you know who this guy is?"

"I'm sorry, I don't?"

"How come you don't know? I told you about him the other day. I told you his story and how I was planning to meet him on the day of our flight."

"Honey, you talk too much and I never listen."

I could hear his ego and manhood breaking into thousands of pieces inside. I was biting my lips so hard not to laugh and make things worse. The last thing I imagined myself doing at the airport was to be between a man and his wife, thinking that is what it's all about—men talk, and women listen only to what they want to. I guess I am going to be a marriage counsellor now, I thought.

I turned to the husband to attempt some damage control. "It's normal for women not to pay attention to what we say sometimes. Their minds are busy with other stuff—the house, kids, cleaning, and their jobs. It's fine, please calm down."

To her: "I am sure you remember, you're just tired from the flight."

It didn't work and the two kept fighting and shouting at each other, with me in the middle. Passengers looked at the three of us strangely, wondering what was going on. I am no expert in relationships, but I could see that this was going to take a while. I decided to run away. "I am sorry but I have to go. I have an interview in two minutes."

I am a thirty-seven-year-old single man and unfortunately I can state that I haven't ever been in love. So sad, I know. Like other guys, I had crushes and girls that I admired. I thought at the time that it was love, but now I know it was not, maybe because I can't remember their names or faces. When I was living at the airport, I found a different kind of love. I fell in love with what I was doing and what I believed in.

At that point, I realized that love is not only what they portray in movies and songs. It's not only about heartbeats, feelings, tears, smiles, relationships or marriages. Love is a human need, a motivator and a great source of power. Real love will never die, and it will keep you going no matter how angry, sad, desperate, weak and lonely you are. Real love will lead you to win in the end and, for the first time, I fell in love with commitment to a cause, surprised by the power a human soul can find at the lowest moments and at the time when they need it the most. Love has a lot to do with that.

I did meet someone special at the airport, however, someone I thought I could fall in love with. I didn't plan for it to happen and I never told anyone about it, not even her. Later, when I was in the Malaysian detention centre I made a promise to myself. I promised that if I ever got out of the prison and met her again, I would tell her.

She was a member of one of the TV crews that visited me at the airport. Very professional, educated and, of course, very beautiful. She tried to keep it professional, but after a while I could see how hard she was trying to hide her tears. She hugged me before saying goodbye, and for the next week all I could think of was Arabic love poetry that reminded me of her.

I look for beauty between the lines of a poem and the paragraphs of a novel; I seek it out in the soundtrack of movies and the notes of a popular song. At Whistler, I was so close to it, surrounded by mountains, lakes, forests and snowfall. I saw it when I watched a bear cross the road, a squirrel climb the stairs, or a pet share my bed. I hear it in my mother's voice on the phone, and see it while watching a video of my nephew, and smell it with my first cup of coffee in the morning. If I close my eyes and listen, then I will hear the knock at the door, and she will be standing there on the other side—smiling, happy, waiting for me to let her in. I will know it's her, as she has a special way of knocking (perhaps she knows how to play the drums), but it will be the faint smell of her perfume that tells me it's really her. When I open the door, I will not speak, hug or kiss her; I will just stand there admiring her beauty with Ed Sheeran, Adele and Celine Dion singing in my mind. The face of a woman with a mind and intelligence and empathy—for me, that is beauty at its most magnificent. Beauty that tells you, you are alive. My feelings for that woman with the TV crew helped remind me that I was still human, that I deserved to live and love.

With every video produced about me, with every chat with journalists and influencers, I imagined myself standing at the side of a lake, with a stone in my hand—I throw the stone in the water and see the circles spreading out on the surface. As the months progressed and the media grew, I stopped seeing myself alone at the edge of the water. Along the shore were people from all over the world, people without faces, throwing stones in the water and creating a wave.

Through my connection to all of these people as @kontar81, from powerful countries and countries I'd never even heard of, I started to feel a new kind of citizenship. The Syrian Hassan was becoming the Global Hassan. The time would come when I would discover the power of this new citizenship.

Chapter Eleven

The Airport Prisoner

AMMAR SENT ME a beautiful engagement photo. He is seated, in profile, looking into the face of Tharaa, who is standing behind him, her hands on his shoulders, her face bent close to his as she gazes joyously into his eyes. We were all so happy for them and wanted them to get married sooner rather than later. Ammar refused; he wanted me to be safe first. I fought it—my life was on hold, and I didn't want my family's life on hold as well. "You are in love and you proposed, you should get married, as simple as that." The simplest solution for problems, even complicated ones, is usually the right one. "You should be celebrating life. It is hurting me that you are holding your life back because of me," I told him during one of the many family phone calls to discuss what he was going to do. Finally, we agreed that he and Tharaa would get married at the beginning of August. I even used my position as big brother, which I rarely did, to call Tharaa's father to ask his permission and blessing for the wedding to go ahead. I had not met Tharaa in person, but she came from a well-known, respected family in Sweida.

Part of me wanted this wedding as a message to the outside world that Syrians, even with families separated and death ever present, refused to die or give up. I might have been living in an airport, with the threat of jail and deportation hanging over me, but our family was growing, and there should be dancing and singing. Nothing should stop us from celebrating life. The hall was booked, the invitations sent out for July 25, and I followed the progress, wanting it to be perfect, even suggesting which songs the bride and groom should dance to.

A week before the big day, I was charging my phone at around 10:00 a.m., wearing some new pajamas the teachers had brought for me (too big, I'm smaller than I look on TV) and trying to keep my long hair out of my eyes as I scrolled through Facebook. A cup of coffee was on the seat beside me, just another normal morning at the airport. Then some disturbing posts from Sweida started to appear in my feed. With the time difference, it was only 4:00 a.m. there. What could be happening at 4:00 a.m.? I was used to reading daily news from Syria, about attacks, casualties here and there; after seven years of war, it wasn't big news, just numbers. Not this time though. Something bad and big was happening, and it was another thirty minutes before I learned what was really going on. ISIS was attacking some of the nearby villages and some suicide bombers had blown themselves up inside the town.

Why couldn't science fiction be real, so I could open a window in time and place to travel back there instantly, no ticket or passport needed? I cursed the war, ISIS, the regime that put the Syrian people in this position of powerlessness and danger. I stood up but did not walk. I was thinking of the villages and the people there. I know them, I know the roads and the houses—it was memory, not imagination. There was no point in asking the normal questions people normally ask in such situations: What happened? Who is responsible? Why did it happen? All that mattered was that it was happening and I needed to focus. There will be time for mourning, but not now, I told myself, it's the time to do something. Like a piece of straw facing a storm, I knew that there was nothing I could do. Our town had been attacked before, but not like this. I grabbed my phone and called my family to warn them. They were awake, hearing explosions and trying to learn what was going on. I was worried the most about Ammar. Knowing him, I was sure he would join others to go protect the villages. How could I tell him not to, when that is what I would be doing if I were there? I told him to stay at home, that he was going to be married in a week. "You need to be careful."

"Yes. Sure," he said, but I knew he would ignore me and go anyway.

While my city was at war, I spent the day hiding under the escalator, reading the news reports, calling my family and praying for it to end. Hours and hours later, they called me: "It's over. We kicked them out." And I started breathing again. Two hundred and fifty-five people were killed that day, mostly while they were sleeping, mostly women and children. Others were gone, kidnapped.

Later that night, Ammar and I spoke and we decided to call off the wedding. "This is too big, the city is too sad. We can't be happy while others are mourning their children."

> @kontar81 August 28, 2018
> I never imagine it will be that hard! 2 great contradicting feeling combined together HAPPINESS/SADNESS, a shy desire to smile/cry. War made the Syrians fall apart around the world, but it couldn't stop our desire in live & love. THIS IS HOW WE RESIST. My little brother's wedding

I sat on the same chair, used the same mug for my coffee, and watched my brother's wedding via Skype. I'd showered and dressed up—I didn't have a suit and tie, but I was wearing jeans and a clean T-shirt. I wanted to act as if I was there, greeting guests, smiling at everyone, passing out food. The internet connection wasn't good, so I couldn't watch the whole thing, but I saw Ammar and Tharaa dancing. I also saw my nephew Medo and my mother smiling. Solaf sent me a stream of photos on WhatsApp and that was more than enough. Sweida, like all Syrian cities, was the city of death and love. Later that night I wrote on a piece of paper:

أولئك الذين يلعبون مع الموت, أكثر من يحب الحياة.

Those who play with death, love life the most.

People call him Nas, but his real name is Nuseir Yassin. He is famous for his daily one-minute videos on Facebook, with millions of followers. He's full of energy, fast, organized and talented with a vision, yet humble and kind.

After almost six months living at the airport, my daily routine was at risk of becoming a comfort zone. Nothing I nor my Avengers were doing seemed to be able to speed up the process of getting the visa for Canada. As the sun rose on Day 169, then 171, then 177, I felt my soul wilt. Nothing was working—not the change.org petition, Canada Caring's lobbying and email campaigns, not the media storm generated by my social media activities. Was my future going to be years under that escalator?

It started with a brief direct message sent via Instagram. "Hey, buddy, I am Nas. I heard about your situation, please send me your mobile number." We had a quick WhatsApp chat, and he said, "I can tell you are trying hard to solve your problem. I want to help."

I believe there was a beauty that existed in my dark story: the support of Laurie and Stephen and Mr. Andrew, working out of the spotlight to bring me to Canada; the empathy and kind messages from hundreds and thousands of people around the world; and the humour behind the life of the new "Terminal Man." But mostly there was the truth—I never lied about any part of my story, as I believed telling the truth would set me free, even if telling it was hard and sometimes shameful, the mistakes I'd made that had brought me to KLIA2. Nas wanted to hear that, not wanting to be involved in a fake story that might backfire on him, for supporting the wrong person. He called me back to fill in the gaps, to hear for himself and connect the dots, and was convinced. "Let us do this."

Nas, who is Palestinian–Israeli and holds an Israeli passport, was not permitted to enter Malaysia so couldn't come to meet me himself. I offered to record whatever he wanted and send it to him, as that is what I'd been doing for international media channels, but that was not his way. He wanted the sound and video quality to be absolutely right and the content consistent with the vision he had for it. So the next day, his friend Agon Hare arrived at KLIA2 at 11:00 a.m. with a camera, cellphone and the script of what we were going to record. I was waiting for him.

Agon, who is originally from Poland, is a very nice, talented guy who always has a smile on his face. He has his own Facebook video blog called Project Nightfall. His plan was to stay at the airport until the next flight to Singapore and shoot the video over the next three hours without passing through immigration or entering Malaysia. We spent most of our time in the toilet because I knew there were no cameras there and the police couldn't see what we were doing. Agon used the camera when we were in the toilet and his phone when we weren't. We were doing our best to hide what we were doing, with Nas calling every fifteen minutes to make sure that everything was going okay. Nas knew his relationship with the Malaysian authorities was strained and had warned me that what we were doing was risky and maybe dangerous. It was risky for Agon too because the authorities might react badly and I didn't know what the police might do if he were caught. But we both agreed that the risk was worth it.

I was relieved when Agon boarded the flight to Singapore. You can breathe now, I thought. The rest is up to them, the editing and the posting. Two and a half days later, on Day 180, Nas called me.

"Get ready. We're going to post it today."

"What do you think, Nas? How many people do you think will watch?" I asked him. "Do you think it might be three, four million?"

"No, I think more like five to six million."

We were both wrong.

At 8:30 p.m., on Friday, September 3, the Nas Daily episode, "The Airport Prisoner" went live.

> This is the unusual story of Hassan Kontar, who has been living in an airport in Malaysia for 6 full months. He has no valid passport or anywhere to go.
> Please watch the video for more details.
> What can you do to help?
> To be honest, our options are quite limited. Hassan refused to accept any money donations.
> So the only thing we can do is raise awareness that this guy...exists. And if you live in Canada, it's even more important to raise awareness there and hopefully try to expedite the application process. Tag relevant authorities or even the prime minister!
> Special thanks to my buddy Project Nightfall for doing the impossible and flying all the way to Malaysia to help me make this video. That was a well executed plan!!

Around 11:00 p.m. that night, I turned off my phone—I could not keep up with all the messages and comments. Knowing the agents and officers would come for me soon, I pretended to sleep. Starting at 1:00 a.m. the first team came, and they kept coming throughout the night, eight different sets of interrogators. I answered them all the same way. "I have no idea who Nas is. He's a guy who came three days ago and told me he has a tourism blog and that is why

I did it. My phone is closed, as you can see. What is going on anyway?"

That night I knew, absolutely, that they'd made the decision to jail me. They wouldn't do it right away. They'd wait because they wouldn't want it to appear as if they were reacting to the video, but they would be coming for me. I sent WhatsApp messages to Laurie, Stephen and some of my other Canadian friends, and another to Dr. Osama. "They are going to arrest me soon. Let us get ready." I also wrote a tweet and saved it as a draft, in case they came and I had no time to write. "I tried, on my way to the airport prison. Thank you all, love you all."

Nas would later take some heat, accused of making money from the hopeless situation of others. It's an accusation often levelled against social media influencers. Some people think only one way— what is the influencer making out of this, how much money? They question motives, spread negativity and conspiracy theories, without considering the huge positive impact for the people who are the subject of the video. Trolls should not stop influencers from working because of fear. Nas was one of the people who changed my life; if he benefited at all, what I got was so much more.

After I arrived in Canada, Nas called to congratulate me and to apologize, as he thought he'd been part of complicating the problem. "Buddy," I told him, "you were part of the solution, a big part, but not a part of the problem. We both knew the risk, and I am the one who agreed to take it."

"The Airport Prisoner" had eighteen million views in three days, and for the next three weeks I waited for them to come. Three of them paid me another visit, with security guards who stood a little too far away to actually protect them. One of them I had met before. He introduced himself as a representative of the Prime Minister's office. Two of them spoke to me while the third kept quiet all the time. That is how I knew that he was the boss.

He asked me to put my cellphone where they could see it to make sure I was not recording. "You are a threat to our national security and a great source of embarrassment to our country," he said.

"Did your investigation lead you to the fact that I'm Bin Laden's first cousin? No! Did you see me manufacturing bombs under the escalator? No! Then what are you talking about?"

"You have three choices," he said. "We can send you back to Syria, put you secretly on a plane to Canada, or send you to jail."

"Are you sure you are from the Prime Minister's office?" I replied. "How a decision-maker could surround himself with people of your limited ability, I will never know. There are no flights to Syria. Airlines will not allow me to board a flight to Canada. That leaves you with only one choice, not three. The only choice you have, and what you really want to do, is to put me in jail. You can do that, but make sure you are prepared for what will come after."

The tension in the air was obvious to me. A few days before the arrest, a journalist from the BBC visited me. Then they showed up. Dressed casually, they distributed themselves throughout the seating area and tried to look like normal passengers, but they never took their eyes off us. I asked the reporter to put away her notebook and pen; I did not want her to get in trouble. She didn't believe me, and I told her about the NBC TV crew to convince her. I asked her to hug me, take a photo and leave.

Dr. Osama called me at the airport while I was waiting. "There was a meeting with the Prime Minister today. He saw some lawyers before the formal meeting began, and there was some chat. He told them, 'Some state officials are not doing their jobs properly. A case like Hassan Al Kontar's should not have been developed and reached the media. It should be finished quickly.'" That was one of my first indications that my arrest was close.

Before Canada, I had only lived under different forms of dictatorships. I'd never voted in my life and wouldn't know what it felt like to go to a polling station. In Syria, we had a referendum every seven years, but most of us never voted as we all knew what the result was going to be. In the UAE, they don't even bother with that. In Malaysia, however, they do have elections and had ended up bringing back a ninety-four-year-old man to govern them again. Maybe they were running out of options, or maybe it was just habit. Either way, he wanted to make an example of me.

The other warning call was from Mr. Andrew. To hear the anxiety in his voice, choosing his words with care as he delivered his message, worried me. "I had a call from a UNHCR employee in Malaysia, and he told me this: 'You should advise Hassan. I know the Malaysian government and they are reaching their limit. He is at risk. They are going to act, and it's going to be bad.'"

"Sir, there is no surprise there," I said. "They are going to act, and they are just using UNHCR to make me afraid, so I'll end it on their terms. I am not going to. They know where to find me the minute they decide to jail or deport me. I will hold my ground no matter what."

"Just be careful and try to cool it down a little," Mr. Andrew advised me.

It never occurred to me to pull back or give up. I was proud of what I was doing. Challenging them was keeping me alive and giving my life a purpose.

No government in the world likes bad PR, and the Malaysian government was reacting defensively, through critical articles in their newspapers and on radio and TV. They were using social media, with a small army of accounts, some clearly fake, to spread rumours, negative comments and attacks about me online, trying to make me doubt myself. I even received threatening private messages, all designed to frighten me.

I read the comments and messages in the beginning, but then I stopped—it felt bad to feel all that hate and anger. No matter what

I did, they weren't going to like me. I was making their country look bad, and when facing an outside enemy, any country will come together, no matter who is right and who is wrong. I was that outside enemy, even though I had tried to avoid criticizing the Malaysian government in the media and to stick to the story of the Syrian war and refugee crisis. But I was stuck at their airport, and that was enough to make them look bad.

I didn't take the threats seriously. As I used to tell myself, barking dogs rarely bite. If you want to kill someone, you go for it—you don't inform your victim first.

Chapter Twelve

Endgame

IT WAS MONDAY night, around 10:00 p.m. I was in my spot under the escalator, reading and drinking coffee. Then, like something out of a movie—a raid on a drug dealer or a terrorist cell—they approached, thirteen of them, the lights from their phone cameras making it hard to see their faces. I smiled and reached for my phone. A tall, thin, aggressive guy came closer and said, "Don't use your cellphone!"

"Am I under arrest?" No answer. He kept quiet, like he was waiting for orders, then, "I need you to come with us."

"Where?" I asked.

Again, no answer. He pointed to my belongings.

"Bring your bags with you."

"Am I under arrest?"

"I have orders, and you need to come with us."

During my early days at the airport, I once tweeted about chocolate. It was a joke, but people took it seriously and were under the impression that I loved chocolate. I don't (I have never had a sweet tooth), and by the time they came, I had an entire suitcase full of chocolate. I left it behind.

"Aren't you going to bring your mattress?" he asked.

"Where to?"

I opened my phone and sent a WhatsApp message to Dr. Osama, not to my family. I couldn't do that to them. We started walking, me pushing the trolley and them walking next to me. Some in front and some behind, in case I decided to run maybe, even though I had nowhere to go.

People were staring at us. We made a very strange sight: me with my flip flops, long hair and beard, pushing a trolley of suitcases and surrounded by police. Where are they taking him? What kind of criminal is he? Some looked afraid. Some looked sorry for me.

They took me to the airport police station. It was walking distance from where I had been, but in a different building, so for the first time in almost seven months I was outside. I was in Malaysia. They were allowing me into the country, just so they could jail me.

They put me in a small room with my bags and phone. They kept the door open to what looked like a staff meeting room with a board on the wall listing the names of the employees and the times of their shifts, and a table and some chairs. The air was full of smoke. They have a habit of smoking inside their offices. It was 11:30 p.m. People would come in to look at me, give me a malicious smile and leave.

There was leftover coffee in my mug, which I drank, wondering when I would have my next cup. I asked if I could smoke and they said no. I asked to go to the bathroom, where I smoked anyway. Then I opened my phone and called Andrew Brouwer. "Sir, it's happening."

At 3:00 a.m., they arrested me.

"Put your hands behind your back!"

I did it without complaining. I knew it was useless to argue with them or even ask what I was being charged with. I could feel their satisfaction at getting their revenge after months of global embarrassment.

It felt strange to be in a car after almost seven months trapped in the airport. God, I totally forgot about cars, I said to myself, but not airplanes. The car was a civilian sedan, dark and cold, but clean, and the road was empty but long. Three officers escorted me to the local police station where they were going to detain me. Being in the backseat with handcuffs made me feel sick, dizzy. The minute they stopped the car and opened the door, I threw up.

"Take off all your clothes."

There are no limits to what a human being with a little power will do when it comes to humiliating others. The man who feels powerful because of his gun is not a man. There is nothing you can do to humiliate the soul. That's what I told myself to stop feeling embarrassed.

When you reach the end, when you are standing on the very cliff edge of danger, the anger you feel inside could move mountains. They want you to lash out, that's why they push you to the limit. They want to turn you into a criminal so they can justify what they are doing to you. It's so damn hard not to. You feel the blood rush to your head. Your eyes open wide and you stop blinking. Your breath is slow and heavy. You can hear it, along with your heart beating. You clench your teeth and your hands automatically form into fists. Your mouth is dry. The animal inside you is snarling for you to attack. When you don't, when you control your anger, it's a small, precious victory.

They gave me a pair of shorts, orange ones. They were so big I had to keep holding onto them, so they wouldn't fall down. But no T-shirt. When I asked for one, they said it was not allowed, so I was naked from the waist up.

"I guess I will be Tarzan for tonight, then." They didn't laugh.

I had no money with me, just my phone, which they took away. I signed their documents and by 4:30 a.m. I was in a cell. All I could think about was my family. Childhood memories, our farm, my parents, watching cartoons with my siblings, my brother's wedding, my nephew. I thought about my mother's tears after my father's death. I thought about being held in detention in UAE and how I had broken my promise to never, ever, be jailed again. I thought about governments, media, interviews, war, Syria and people around the globe.

I forced myself to try to remember some of the messages that I had received during my time at the airport or the names of the people who sent them. These happy memories would take me away from my reality, to a happy world where I could forget where I was or what was awaiting me. Should I ask to call my family? Or Laurie? I couldn't do it. Sadness can wait, I thought. Let them sleep well tonight.

During our WhatsApp chats, I'd nicknamed Laurie "007"—she seemed to have the ability to know everything. There I was, curled up with my head to my knees, feeling cold, and I looked at the wall. Someone had written "0007." I laughed. "God, you are here too!" It turned out to be the name of a local gang, but I took it as a sign. I wanted to—it felt nice and gave me hope. I spent the hours before dawn trying to fit my body into those too-big shorts; the cell was so cold and full of mosquitoes. It made me think of Chandler, making fun of Monica's bathing suit. "Oh, I thought that was what they used to cover Connecticut when it rained." Are you for real? There I was—sick, dizzy, cold, half-naked and with a stomach ache—but remembering an episode of *Friends* made me smile. The shorts were so big, but not big enough. Focus, goddammit, I thought, then I smiled as I realized I *was* focusing. At that moment, I needed to mock life. I needed to remind myself that there was a happy future beyond these bars and to see in my mind's eye not the cold, aggressive faces of my jailers, but those of the people who supported and cared about me. They will get me out of here, I thought, and they want you to keep smiling.

That night, I reminded myself that being afraid doesn't mean being weak. There is a difference. Being afraid is a natural human response, and there is nothing we can do about it, but there is a lot we can do to not be weak. Fear reminds you not to deny your situation, and to find the courage to face it. Weakness is a behaviour, a choice, a decision. In that cell, I felt afraid but not weak.

Two hours later, the sun was up and I could see my new home properly.

It was a small room, two metres by two metres, and one part of the floor was higher than the other. I figured it was the sleeping area because two men occupied it although there was barely enough space. I was seated next to the door. No blankets, sheets or pillows, just cold, brownish-green, smooth cement.

In one of the corners, next to the sleeping guys, was the "bathroom"—a hole in the ground with no walls to give you any kind of privacy. There was a bucket of water under a leaky tap. The sound of droplets plunking into the bucket broke the silence, along with the snoring of one of the guys. The dripping tap must have driven someone crazy as there was a torn piece of orange shorts wrapped around the tap. But it kept leaking anyway.

The prison cells were arranged in a square, looking out at a barred area in the centre with no roof overhead. It could be worse, I said to myself. I've had no fresh air for seven months and now I can have it all for me. Later that day it would rain and I would change my mind.

Around 7:00 a.m., keys turned in the cell door. Breakfast was served: some sweet biscuits and a glass of pink-coloured water. Ten minutes later, they called my name.

"You are going to court."

There were around twelve of us in one long chain, handcuffed together. I couldn't find my flip flops—"Must be one of the prisoners," they said—so my feet were bare. Now I am definitely Tarzan, I thought. They loaded us into the back of a truck and I forced myself not to throw up for the next thirty minutes, the time it took to reach the court.

"Can I know my charges, please, so I can prepare my defence before I see the judge?"

The answer was both shocking and funny: "We are working on it."

I smiled big time. "Let me know once you figure it out."

They locked us all up in one big cell, with prisoners from other jails. One at a time, the other prisoners were taken out of the cell to see the judge, but not me. It was a heavy, slow time, especially when I thought about life outside these walls—there were people right then who were walking on the streets, going to their jobs, eating, drinking. They had the right to because they were not criminals, but neither was I.

Around 1:00 p.m., an officer came. "Al Kontar. Hassan Al Kontar." All the guards were looking at me as if they knew who I was, but they kept their distance.

"You are not going to see the judge today," he said, "maybe tomorrow."

Later that day, around six and back at my cell, one of the police guards asked me, "What are you here for?"

"It's a long story," I said. "But I don't know why I am *here* exactly."

"That is easy," he answered and left. Five minutes later he was back.

"Marijuana."

"Huh! What?"

"Marijuana. You are here for marijuana possession."

"You must be mistaken."

"No, it's written in your file."

Drug possession in Malaysia is a very serious crime, and you can end up behind bars for many years for possessing just a few grams. What I didn't know at that time was that he was trying to intimidate me, and was using this as a ploy to open a conversation, to get what he was really after. "I am very sure, but I will check your file again. Anyway, I will be here tonight so let me know if you want something."

"Please do check and yes I want something else."

"What?"

"I want to make a phone call."

"That is not allowed. We can make it work if . . . you know."

He started moving the fingers of his right hand as if he were counting money.

"I don't have any money here, but I can get it if you allow me to make a phone call. I will get someone to transfer it to your account."

That was all it took for him to open the door and escort me to his office. I asked for a cigarette and he gave me one, which I smoked while he went to get the phone. When he came back, I said, "Let us agree first. I need to be moved to a cell where I can be alone, a full pack of cigarettes and a lot, a lot of coffee."

"Make the call. It will cost you 400 ringgit."

"200?"

"350."

"300, and that is all I have."

"Okay, but if my partner asks you, say it was 200."

He was not only a corrupt police officer, he was a thief, stealing his partner's share. I agreed and called Dr. Osama. He was worried and had been trying to learn where I was and what was going on. I asked him to call my family and my Canadian friends, to let them know that I was fine. In the thirty seconds left from the one-minute call the officer allowed me, I asked Osama to transfer the money. He knew what it was for. "Money talks, buddy." I'm sure he was smiling like me. Two minutes later, the transfer was complete. That night the jail was more like a resort than a prison. Others might have asked for KFC or McDonald's meals; me, I went on my own to the farthest cell, with a pack of Marlboro Red King Size and a full pitcher of coffee. Like the Arab prince from long ago, who was drinking when told his father the king had been killed and said, "Today I drink, tomorrow I act," I was going to enjoy what I had, and start the war tomorrow.

For the next two days, nothing much happened except the normal routine investigation visits during the day, and a trip to a different police centre where they took my fingerprints and some photos for my criminal record. In addition to the usual questions I was accustomed to answering, they asked weird ones, that made no sense at all. How my father's middle name and my mother's hometown, or my brother-in-law's last name were related to my case, I had no idea. They asked them anyway, all of them, starting from the day my parents and siblings were born, up to the day I was arrested. They were trying hard to tie me to a crime, any crime, so they were digging anywhere and in all directions with the hope that they might find something that would get them off the hook with the media.

They didn't take me back to court again, which was a relief as I'd hated the way they handcuffed us, the truck they used to transport us, and the crowded holding cell. At night, I tried to sleep on the floor with mosquitoes swarming around and nothing to cover myself with. When I couldn't sleep, I'd sit up and wait for the police officer who liked bribes to come, but he never showed up after that second night.

October was not a good month for me. On October 2, 2017, I had gone into the UAE detention centre for the second time. Now, a year later, I was in a Malaysian jail. They started "visiting" me on Day One: people call them police, immigration, intelligence, security service, but I called them the "bats." They are nocturnal, active at night, and love to wake you up at 2:00 a.m. to ask the same questions each and every time.

During one of the many interrogations, I said to the officer, "How come I am inside Malaysia? I thought I was banned from entering the country?"

"We issued you a special pass and lifted the ban."

"So, you are able to lift the ban to jail me, but not to allow me into the country. Is that legal?"

"Yes, it is. The police arrested you, not immigration."

"The police! Is that why it took you three weeks to arrest me? You were making a plan. Am I a criminal now?"

"We'll see."

While I was in police custody, I learned that Malaysians didn't like Nas much, and his video about me had been the last straw on their camel's back. That he'd made Singapore his work base, with all the historical issues between the two countries, made things worse. One of the officers, during an interrogation, mocked me. "Where is Nas now? Let him help you!"

I spent four days in the custody of the police and believed that was the worst that could happen, but I was wrong again. On the fifth day, my case officer—the only one who'd showed some empathy—came and said, "Nothing, nothing to charge you with, you are no criminal. I even went to the deputy general attorney to explain your situation, and how you can't remain in our custody as we have nothing to charge you with. He agreed to transfer you to the immigration department." This policeman was short and young, with a hint of cleverness and the threat that he could be dangerous if he needed to be.

I smiled. "You may not be aware, but this was the plan from the beginning. To arrest me and then transfer me to immigration jail was the plan. When?"

He smiled. "Now. I am going to take you to my office and drive you there. It's a little bit far."

In his office, he told them to remove the handcuffs. I returned their shorts to them and was allowed to change into my own jeans and sweater; these would be the only clothes I would have at the immigration jail. After I had changed, he took me to a small kitchen. He asked me to sit, made a cup of coffee and gave me a cigarette. We chatted for almost two hours; his team members came in and out, but he was clearly the senior man. The only thing I remember him saying was, "You know, they are tigers. But I asked them not to be with you."

The drive to the immigration jail took forty minutes. "We chose this detention centre because it is the best one. The same as we took you to the best police station from the airport." What he was really saying was, "When the time comes, don't forget that we are treating you well." What I was thinking was, if this is your best, God help those who are in other places—what do they look like and what goes on there?

Later I would hear horrible stories from other prisoners, and how much happier they were to be where I was. "You really don't want to be *there*," they used to say to me.

Before he handed me over to the immigration officers, my case officer brought out his phone and took a selfie with me. Then he explained who I was and why I'd been transferred. A woman, medium-ranking from her uniform, said, "We need to be careful with this one." They processed me for two hours, opening a new file, taking new fingerprints and new photos. Then they took off my handcuffs and sent me to the basement, where the cells were.

The basement was clean and air-conditioner cold, giving the impression that it was a new building that they were trying to take care of before time tore it apart. There was another reason for keeping it clean—human rights organizations, UN officials, media, consular staff, they were all making official visits there, and the Malaysian authorities wanted to make a good impression and show they were taking care of the inmates. The corridors were long and narrow and there were only two large cells, one for men, one for women. There were administration offices and dormitories for the guards, who were on shift two days in a row. On the walls were signs listing the rules and telling us how to behave.

At reception, they'd taken our bags and all our belongings, leaving us with only the clothes we were wearing. The way they spoke to us, the way they searched my bags, the way they looked at me, all of this I was used to. I was the enemy, and they were the protectors of their country, a country I had offended. It was annoying that they wouldn't let me take my hygiene products and toothbrush. "You can buy new ones from us," they said, another way to make money. Since I had none, I would use my fingers to clean my teeth and cellmates shared their soap and shampoo. What was new was they took my eyeglasses, leaving me half-blind for two months.

There was another difference, too. They had their authority and power, the guns and the keys, but I had my own army, my Avengers and my supporters, and that would give me some protection. There was no physical abuse towards me during the time I spent there, unlike other prisoners, just mental and emotional abuse, which was nothing new. I'd seen it all before and it became more like a joke to me and a way to break the daily routine with some suspense. I believe they'd been given instructions to be careful around me.

It was a Friday, 6:00 p.m., when I first entered the cell for men. One of my cellmates was from Nigeria, a DJ who'd overstayed his visa, who was there with another Nigerian and a man from South Sudan. He'd been there for a week before I arrived and he knew who I was. The cell was overcrowded, with no place to sit, sleep or walk around. The Nigerian smiled at me and asked his friends to make some room for me with them. I was a fresh face, a new story and would help pass the time. He introduced me and after he told them about me, the other two remembered hearing my story and began to fire their questions at me.

The first nights were the hardest, trying to adjust to another new reality. During the day there was nothing much to do, and at night it was hard to sleep—no space to lie down, the lights always on, the floor cold and the smell coming from the open toilet. I did as the others, leaned against the wall, with my head on my knees and my hands inside my sweater, always with an eye open to see if a better space became available. In twenty days, I would have my own space, as I was one of the senior inmates, the others having gone.

For the next three days, nothing happened, until Monday morning, when they called me for another interrogation. Unlike the other inmates, who had routine investigations in one of the offices in the basement—just some forms to fill and some questions to answer—I went upstairs to the main office, escorted in handcuffs by two guards. There were three officials waiting, two were wearing civilian clothes and one a uniform with stars on his shoulders. They invited me to sit in the empty chair and began asking the same questions I'd been answering for the last seven months. It took them two hours to finish, with one of them typing everything on a computer. They added some lines to the end of my statement, saying I thanked the Malaysian government, then told me to sign.

"What next?" I asked.

"We'll let you know."

Wake up at 5:30 a.m., get in line for breakfast: two pieces of toast and tea in a plastic bag. Eat toast, drink tea, clean bag, fill with water, turn it into a pillow. No common language with most of the inmates, no topics to talk about with those who speak English. No TV, no books, no phone calls. The rhythm of life was mealtimes. Noon: some rice wrapped with paper, with a piece of chicken, fish or Tofu, depending on the day (we learned the menu schedule quickly). Eat lunch, clean the paper to make a blindfold to cover our eyes; try to sleep. Last meal, 4:30: more paper-wrapped rice parcels and an egg or chicken (depending on the day). The guards would enter the cell twice a week to destroy our "pillows," emptying them on the floor where we sat. There'd be some shouting, some yelling, then they'd leave and we'd wait for the next meal.

The Nigerian guys were some company and switched their places with me during the night. For a week, nothing happened, just the endless waiting. I had no idea what was going on outside: was there any progress? Had they forgotten about me? How was my family? I'd walk forward and backwards, just a few steps as there was so little space to move. A few minutes of that exercise would calm me, and I would remember to smile, knowing my friends were doing everything they could, I was sure of it. Then I'd sit down again and try to have a conversation with my cellmates.

During those days, my old cellmates left and were replaced by new ones, and I became one of the elders. Like the other prisons I'd been in, that meant I had the right to a spot to sleep and could stand nearer to the front of the line for meals—the privileges of rank. The other prisoners noticed how the guards kept their distance from me, but not from them, so they knew there was something different about me and would ask me to resolve problems, such as management of the sleeping spaces. At night, I would sit with some and ask them to tell me their stories, where they were from, what their villages were like, their traditions, food and way of life.

One day, the cell door opened and a young man entered who looked slightly familiar. He was in his early twenties, slim and with a stylish haircut, wearing only shorts and a T-shirt. Someone new to talk to I cheered inwardly. He was from Morocco and seemed in shock, lost and afraid, so I talked to him, answered his questions and tried to calm him down. "Everything is going to be all right," I repeated. "Don't be afraid. It's a matter of a few days and then you will be home again." It took him a few days, he was quiet at first, but he began to think of me as his safety net and opened up. We'd eat together, share our food, and I would try to cheer him up.

I asked him some questions about Morocco, and quickly learned he didn't have much education and confused the current king with his father. Okay, so no politics or history then, I thought. But it was the same with sports and movies. There must be something we could talk about. Work! I'll ask him about his work. "I make pizzas in a restaurant," he said. So, for the one month that he was in the detention centre, I'd talk to him for a few minutes in the day and say, "Tell me again, how do you make pizza dough?" When I got bored of talking about pizzas, I'd ask him about Moroccan tea and what they ate at their weddings. He was from a poor family with a hard life, who'd travelled abroad to help as best he could. It wasn't prison that was bothering him, it was going back to his family with no money. "I am good at what I am doing, I just need a chance," he'd say. I tried to boost his morale—tell him to keep moving, never give up hope—but whenever I began to sound too preachy, I would poke his shoulder and say, "I keep forgetting about this damn pizza dough. How do you make it again?"

It was at this Malaysian detention centre that I met Uyghurs for the first time. I'd heard of them but had never met one in person. Uyghurs are a Muslim minority persecuted by the Chinese government, who face arrest and death on a daily basis, with the government trying to prevent news of them from reaching the ears of the world. Five of them came one day, and at first we thought they were Chinese, waiting to be deported to China. None of them spoke English, so I didn't pay much attention to them. Then I saw one of the guards pointing at them and heard the word "Uyghurs." I knew that if they were sent back to China, they would most likely die, or at least be arrested. I watched them as they slept during the night, their cold bodies shivering, and forgot about my problems. How much injustice and ignorance do we need to fight? What sin had these men committed? Two days later the guards took them away. Later, I asked one what had happened to them. He told me they'd been sent to Turkey and he didn't know why, that was just the order. For me, it made sense—historically, they were part of the Ottoman Empire, with Turkish roots. So the Turkish government was welcoming them as their own. I smiled, as I knew they were going to be safe, but I couldn't stop myself from adding one comment, which the guard did not get or understand, "I hope they are not going to use them the way they are using the Syrian refugees."

There were twelve days with no interrogations or meetings, and then on a Tuesday, someone called my name through the cell door bars. It wasn't a guard, but one of the people from upstairs, an immigration department employee. "I just came to tell you that next Thursday, at 2:00 p.m., a man from the Canadian High Commission is going to visit you. Make yourself ready."

They'd done it! They'd been working on it and hadn't forgotten about me. Things were happening! Even my eyes were smiling. Canada was closer than ever now, and if it needed me to wait, then that was what I was going to do. My cellmates asked me what the official wanted but I said nothing and did not share with them what was happening. I did not want them to feel worse about themselves; I was a man with the hope of being in a great country, and they had nothing. All they'd done was to have the misfortune of being born on the wrong side of the world, and they deserved a better life. It did not seem right, nor would it help to share news of my good fortune with them.

On Wednesday, I washed my only clothes and stood for six hours so they could dry on me. The next morning, I washed and waited: 2:00 p.m., 3:00, 4:00. Nothing happened, no one came. I made up reasons in my mind—his car broke down, the traffic is bad, he had another meeting, he went to the wrong jail. With no excuses left, I decided the immigration officer had got the day wrong. The man from the Canadian High Commission would come tomorrow. For the next twenty-five days, every day at 2:00 p.m., I stood next to the bars, looked at the basement door and willed the Canadian man to come through it.

While I waited, things were beginning to happen. My lawyer Andrew had appointed a lawyer in Malaysia to help me, and he would come to the jail to give me updates. Getting me to Canada was not an easy task for my Avengers, and there were a lot of technical issues that needed to be sorted before I could go: an interview, fingerprints, photos, questions I needed to answer, papers to be signed, travel documents and tickets, most of which were nearly impossible to arrange while I was still in prison. That didn't stop me from dreaming that each time the key turned in the lock, it would be a guard come to call my name and say my flight was going to be in four hours.

I'd been arrested on October 1, so didn't know what had happened the day after, on October 2, 2018, until about halfway through my imprisonment, when the Malaysian lawyer visited the jail to check on how I was doing. At the end of our one-hour meeting, I asked, "What is going on in the outside world? Any news? Anything about Syria?"

"You know, the world is busy with the murder of the Saudi journalist."

"What journalist? Who?"

"Jamal Khashoggi."

I felt cold, more than usual, but began to sweat. I couldn't look at the lawyer. I was silent, and the lawyer was confused by my reaction. "I don't know too many details," he said, not wanting to make the situation worse. "Just that he is dead. They killed him." It was awkward, and he stood up, getting ready to leave. "I am sorry, I thought you knew. I regret telling you."

Back in the overcrowded cell, I mourned what felt like a personal loss. This was a man I'd known for months, admired for years. I could not sit or sleep. I went to the open cold shower we had in the cell, and stood under it, wearing the only clothes we were permitted to have.

ENDGAME

Twice I witnessed what the system did to weak people, those with no voice, no rights and no embassies to back them up: first in Abu Dhabi, then again in the Kuala Lumpur immigration jail.

About midway through my time in the Malaysian jail, the two locks on the big rusty barred door snapped open to welcome a new guest. He looked like a diminutive man—I couldn't see him clearly without my glasses—but I could make out an orange T-shirt with some sort of logo and black pants. The cell was already overcrowded, with more than forty of us in the three-by-five-metre room—no wonder there was no space to walk, sleep or even sit properly.

Nice! More people, like we don't have enough! I said to myself as I walked toward him, trying to avoid tripping over legs and bodies. Wait, this can't be true! It was not a small man, but a boy. A kid. Thin and short and clearly still in his growing years.

He was standing there, wearing the uniform T-shirt of the restaurant he'd been working in when they arrested him. Not afraid, not shivering, but steady, breathing regularly and calmly, moving his eyes around to check everything out—the room and us—in a way that suggested, young as he was, that he already had experience as a prisoner. Some of the guys from Asia, Bangladesh and Pakistan, were able to communicate with him; they told me he was twelve years old.

During the following days, I kept my eyes on the little one, as I called him. We never spoke, as we had no common tongue between us. He used the plastic bags they brought our tea in as socks or wrapped them around his arms like sleeves in the hope they would bring some warmth. The other prisoners, like me, felt sorry for him. They didn't know what to do other than share their food with him and give him space to sleep.

I didn't need to hear him tell his story, his eyes said it all. When I looked at him during the night, I spoke silently to him. How much has life tested you, little one? I know for sure that you feel betrayed by everyone: by organizations, states, governments, humanity, the law. Even your parents betrayed you, by bringing you into this life, into the wrong time and wrong place.

That was the first time I ever meet a Rohingya and glimpsed a small shred of their tragedy. They are a people without a home. Declared stateless and slaughtered in their home country of Myanmar. A million of them kept in refugee camps in Bangladesh, where they are denied education and human rights, the women facing sexual assault and murder. Even with family members in countries like Canada trying to sponsor them, they are denied exit visas. There are thousands and thousands more in detention centres in Indonesia and Malaysia, where many babies are born stateless. The UNHCR, which is supposed to be taking care of them, instead tells them they shouldn't hope for better.

Ten days after I met him, the little one was transported to a Malaysian refugee camp for the Rohingya. He's probably still there, stockpiled, another lifelong hostage of a failed system and an uncaring world.

The two times I was in prison in the UAE, I worried about my family, the shame of letting them down eating me alive. Inside the Malaysian jail, however, I had the relief of knowing that a group of people I'd never met were giving them support. Unlike some of the media, Laurie, Stephen, Mr. Andrew and Dr. Osama weren't trying to use me or take advantage of my situation. They were my selfless, generous Avengers, so it did not surprise me to hear that they were in daily contact with my family during the two months I was in jail. My Avengers became friends and part of the family, and whenever my mother could not sleep it was enough for her to speak to one of them to relax a little bit, hearing that they were working on it. They are no longer weak, hopeless and alone, I told myself, when the guards pushed me back in the cell and closed the door. If I had achieved nothing during this battle on a personal level, at least I'd given my family new friends around the world to look after them. Knowing that my Avengers were there for my family no matter what was enough to keep me focused and give me strength.

Phone calls were not permitted. The only time the authorities would allow you to make one was if you needed to call someone to get the money for your return ticket. Visits weren't allowed either, but I was an exception. I was an embarrassing problem for them, a problem they wanted to solve without losing face, but they did not know how and were waiting for me to provide them with the solution. Not only was international attention focused on the Malaysian authorities, local media and human rights groups were also keeping an eye on my situation; it was even discussed in parliament. At the beginning of the second month, two men I'd never seen before came down to the basement and called out my name. They handcuffed me and escorted me to the second floor. This was not the normal procedure and meant they had signed me out of the prison guards' custody and into immigration custody. As we rode up the elevator, I thought, he's finally here, the employee from the Canadian High Commission, it could not be anything else. They don't want him to see the basement or the cells, so they've given him an office upstairs for our meeting.

I was wrong. When I entered the room, a high-ranking Malaysian immigration officer was sitting on a chair waiting for me. He invited me to sit next to him and start talking. "We received a call from the Syrian Embassy."

"Twenty days ago I was told that the Canadian High Commission is going to visit. Any updates?"

"I am speaking to you about the Syrian Embassy now!"

"I heard you. I know what they asked you for, but I don't know what your reply was."

"We are a neutral state, and we don't want to jeopardize our relations with them."

"We've been in a war for seven years now. The whole world is cutting their relations with the Syrian regime, but you are telling me that you don't want to jeopardize your relations with them! It's your right, of course, as a country, but are you willing to jeopardize your relations with the rest of the world because of it?"

"They are offering to take you back. The decision has not been made yet but we are looking into it."

"It's a long way to Syria—multiple airlines and airports. A lot of things could happen."

"What do you mean?"

I decided not to give a direct answer. "I know your government wants to solve the problem and for this to end as soon as possible. Make no mistake—deporting me will create more problems and just delay the solution."

"That is it for now."

I was terrified, even though I'd just played tough with him. I didn't know if the Syrian Embassy had really called or not, although I had a feeling that they had, but I also felt that the Malaysian government had no will to deport me, at least not yet. The officer had met with me because they hoped jail had broken me and that I would say, "Yes. I will go back to Syria." Then there'd be no blame and they could claim they were just following my wishes. It would be a win-win situation for them: problem solved, no casualties. But I said no, and so he sent me back to my cell and I never saw him again.

Just a couple of days after this meeting, I received two visits on the same day. The first one was from my Malaysian lawyer, and the second was from two people representing a local human rights office that reported to the Malaysian parliament. The manager of this organization had visited me while I was at the police station, but these two employees had no actual power and were just following up. Their visit, although it wasn't going to result in anything, meant a lot to me. It demonstrated support for me to the Malaysian government, saying "He is not alone and you need to remember that." I was just one person, one man who was saying no, fighting the injustice and asking for his rights from behind bars. That I might set an example for others was the Malaysian government's worry. They might hold the keys, but I had my global citizenship, real help from individuals and worldwide media attention.

The first week of my second month in custody, without any advance notice, the guards called my name around 10:00 a.m. They unlocked the cell door and asked me to come out. My long hair was tied up with an elastic band from one of our food parcels, and I hadn't washed. They handcuffed me and walked me three metres down the hallway to a closed office door, then took off the handcuffs. They knocked on the door, I entered, and there he was, the employee from the Canadian High Commission.

I was smiling so much that he—firm, serious and professional—couldn't resist smiling back.

"How are you doing?" he asked.

"Well, it's not 2:00 p.m. yet, but I am doing fine."

His eyebrow went up. "What do you mean it's not 2:00 p.m.?"

"I have been waiting for you at 2:00 p.m. every day for weeks. That is the time they told me you would come. But it doesn't matter now. You are finally here."

The guards left us alone in the room, just the two of us. The Canadian representative shook my hand, asked me to sit, and so the beginning of the end began.

"It's true. The first time we asked to come was Thursday at 2:00 p.m. But the Malaysian authorities wanted a representative from their government to attend the interview. We said no. That is against the law—it should be confidential."

Looking pointedly up to the corner of the room at the security camera, I said, "I wonder what made them change their minds? If we search carefully, we might find the mic too."

I was hoping he would go easy with me, but that was not how the interview went. Rules were rules, this was his job, and he needed to make sure that everything I said before and now was the truth. He did not express it directly but I felt his empathy. "Whatever you do, don't lie to me," he said.

I pointed to the fingerprint scanner. "I'm familiar with that," I said.

"Are you?"

"Yes."

"Where?"

"I have not lied about my situation on social media or in interviews with journalists, and I am not about to start now. In jail."

"You have been in jail before?"

"Yes. Both in Malaysia and before that in the United Arab Emirates."

"In the Emirates? What for?"

"Financial cases and immigration detention."

He smiled. He knew that already but wanted to hear it from me, to make sure I wouldn't try to hide it. It was a test to see if I would tell the truth or lie to him. Only then did he begin the interview properly and, for the next two hours, he asked me about everything, so much so that it felt like he was squeezing my life out of me.

The guards opened the door. "Sir, it's taking you so long and we need to change the shift."

I also felt it was taking too long, but I was feeling happy and did not want him to leave. If only I could ask him to take me with him rather than going back to my cell to wait again, I thought, but I knew that was not how this worked. I was okay with it. For the last eight months, I'd been waiting for this, and if they wanted me to wait longer, I would. So many believe that the Canadian authorities went easy on me, or skipped steps, but they did not. They did everything by the book, just faster than usual.

"What next?" I asked before he left.

"I am going to study your file. If you are approved, we will send you for a medical exam."

When? I wanted to ask but didn't. Better not to push him, give him time to do his work.

When they took me back to my cell after the interview, I contemplated what was it that would make a country, to which you had no ties at all, change their normal procedures, including shifting all their office equipment—fingerprint scanners, cameras, laptops, microphones—to meet you in jail. What made them submit the request to another government and wait for their approval, to negotiate with them, with all the emails, calls, time and efforts required to do so? Who paid for the travel expenses for that Canadian to come from Singapore, just to meet me? I wished I had my cellphone with me at that moment. It would have been the perfect time to start googling Canada, Vancouver and Whistler, something I'd refused to do the whole time I was at the airport. It seemed like tempting fate and I hadn't allowed myself even one quick online browse, in case my dream did not happen.

Two days after the Canadian interview, while I was standing next to the cell door, holding the cold bars, trying to see the time on the clock hanging on the opposite wall, which was impossible without my glasses, a middle-ranking guard approached me. This was the same guard who always said no when I asked for my glasses back, no when I asked for a headache pill or a blanket, and who threw plastic bags of tea at prisoners if he didn't like the way they spoke to him at mealtimes, wanting them to shout "Yes, sir, thank you, sir" so he could feel the respect he needed. He looked to see if any of his colleagues were watching and then he smiled at me.

"I have always been good to you, haven't I?" he said.

I nodded my head, curious. What did he want from me? This was an opportunity to test my theory about the guards.

"I wanted to ask you something."

"Me! What can the guy behind the bars do for the guy who has the keys?"

"The Canadian immigration officer . . . "

I was bored and I thought this was a way to make the time go faster, so I acted like I had no idea what he was talking about. I wanted to make him feel the control shifting and to understand that his acting was fooling no one.

"Who?"

"You know! The one who visited you here."

"When?"

"Two days ago! The one from the Canadian High Commission."

"Oh, yeah. Nice dude. What about him?"

"Did he ask you about your profession?"

"I can't tell you—he made me swear not to tell anybody about my interview."

"Swear? How?"

"Like this: 'I swear to you, sir.'"

"You know, I have some cousins and friends there."

"Where?"

"In Canada."

I could see how hard he was trying to control himself, not to shout at my stupid answers, trying to be polite and cool with his questions, and me knowing what he was really after from his first question. I was enjoying this, especially as he kept looking right and left to make sure no one was watching.

"Do you want to go there?" I asked him.

"Is there a way? You know, it's Canada!"

"Yeah, tell me about it. It must be hard for you, knowing that your cousins are living a good life while you are in this cold basement. Guarding people like me is probably as far as you'll get in life. You must be envying them."

For once, the jailer wished to be in the place of the prisoner—me.

"Do you think if I applied, they will ask about my job as a police officer?"

"Why? You think you did something wrong as a police officer?"

"No, no. I am just asking."

"They will, but you are a very nice guy. I am sure your record is clear, and that you haven't violated anyone's human rights. They care about these things in Canada, you know."

It got him hard. The words "violation and human rights" hit him hard, and his eyes widened and filled with anger. They flicked from needy to evil.

"Don't stand next to the door! Go and sit over there."

Welcome back, I wanted to say to him, but realized I shouldn't provoke him any further—I'd just smashed his dream. Instead, I asked him what time it was.

"I don't know," he snapped. "Just go and sit."

The man had just made my day. I went and joined the guys, who were curious as to why that particular guard had been chatting to me. So I told them it was a story of people who are thrilled by the little power they have in their hands, but no one understood what I was talking about.

Many long, slow days followed, with me hoping the next would be my last. Fifteen days later they came, four of them with their handcuffs. They put me in a car and took me for the medical exam.

"It is an eighteen to twenty-hour flight, are you mentally stable enough to do it?" the doctor asked me during the thorough medical, which included my least favourite, needles and vaccines.

I laughed. "Doctor, it's been a long day, with four guards watching me, handcuffing and unhandcuffing between every room I enter and exit. I feel dizzy and nauseated, but I have not gone crazy yet. I am no threat to the passengers or the plane. Please write that down and sign my documents so I can go back to my cell."

He did, but not before they rechecked my blood pressure, which had been above the acceptable level. "Do you really expect my blood pressure to be normal?" I asked. "Look at me and where I am coming from! I would be worried and surprised if it was not high."

They ignored this and made me sit, gave me a glass of water and asked me to breathe steadily. Thirty minutes later, they checked it again and I passed. I don't know if I passed because it was normal again or if they just wanted me gone. By midday I was in the car again, on my way back to jail, and I was glad. Not glad to be on my way to the cell again, but happy at the thought that this was going to be one of my last days accompanied by these guards. As I looked through the car window at Kuala Lumpur and the twin towers, it was as if I was trying to save it all in my memory to bid farewell to it. Maybe my flight will be at night, and I will not be able to see this again, I thought. Let me say goodbye now.

"Don't forget us and how good we were to you," one of the guards said during the trip back to the detention jail. "You are going to be in Canada." He took his phone out of his pocket, searched for my name on Facebook and sent me a friend request. Then he took a selfie with me. There I was, handcuffed in the cargo area of the car, with no way out, and he asked me to smile for the selfie.

How can I ever forget about you, I thought, as we parked in front of a local shop and I watched them get something to eat and drink, then smoke a cigarette while they left me locked inside the car. I remembered that big world map at KLIA2, the one I felt was mocking me when I stood next to it. This time it did not say, "I am big, but I have no place for you." This time, as my mind's eye zoomed to Malaysia on the map, it said, "We don't like you, the majority of us, so don't come back." All the hate messages and comments I received from Malaysians crossed my memory like a newsreel.

For three days I refused to take off the patches that covered the spots where they'd taken the blood samples and given me the injections. They were a reminder that the end was close. I thought I might even keep them on until I was on the plane to Canada.

Some of my cellmates asked what was going on, with all the movement and interviews, but as before, I refused to talk about it. To be jealous of each other, and to want the best for ourselves, is a part of our human nature. It doesn't make you a bad person to ask, "Why him but not me?" It is a reasonable question, as we all should have the same rights. It was hard to look them in the eyes and feel what they were going through, and what was waiting for them. My tragedy was about to end. I was travelling to a great country with a promising future ahead of me—but what about them? All they'd done was to borrow money or sell their land or home, to pay for a visa that then expired, and now they were being sent home, to face debt with no future.

On Day 55 of my Malaysian jail time, a female officer passed in front of my cell, just before the end of the official week's working hours. It was Thursday, and the next two days were holidays, with no employees or officers to answer your questions, just the guards on duty. She saw me standing next to the bars, walked on for three or four paces, then turned back and stood in front of me.

"Monday, you are going back to your country." I was shocked. Was that true? Had I understood her correctly? We didn't trust each other, certainly, but was that enough of a reason for me to ignore what she'd just said? I didn't know what was going on outside. Had my application been rejected? Did I fail the medical exam? I went over the interview with the Canadian High Commission official, question by question, answer by answer—what had I done wrong? Was that why the Malaysians were deporting me to Syria? Because the Canadians had informed them that my application had been rejected? Or maybe she was wrong and meant my flight to Canada? Or was she just bored and decided to play some mind games with me? For the rest of that day, I stood next to the bars waiting. If it was her shift, she might come back again and I could check with her what she meant. But she never did.

For two days, I boiled inside, not knowing what was going on, and why she'd said what she said. I was losing it, pacing in the cell, speaking to know one, walking on the spot, not eating or sleeping. That female officer's face and words burned in my mind. I hated her and hated the kind of power and authority she had that allowed her to play with people's feelings and lives without taking any responsibility for her words.

This woman was like the immigration police officer who'd driven me to Abu Dhabi airport, the Turkish Airline supervisor who'd cancelled my ticket, the Cambodian authorities who refused me entry, the Syrian Embassy that wouldn't renew my passport and the Malaysian authorities all the time. Small people with little authority, who used their power to make themselves feel superior to those weaker than themselves. They try to force respect through fear, to make themselves feel more important. But if they need something from you, they switch from tigers to lambs, and there is some consolation in seeing the need in their eyes.

On Sunday, at last, I saw a familiar face, the same guy who took the selfie with me in the police car. "You have no idea how big a mistake you are making and what might happen because of it," I said through the bars to him.

"What do you mean?"

"You don't know?"

"No."

"Well, I still have one day before you send me back to my country and who knows what may happen in the next twenty-four hours."

"Who told you that you are going back to your country? And what do you mean by who knows what may happen in the next hours? Are you planning on doing something?"

"A female officer came two days ago and told me that you will send me back to my country on Monday morning. Do me a favour and pass all of our conversation to your superiors, please. All of it."

"Okay, but you do nothing until I do so."

He thought I might harm myself in my cell, and that was my plan. I would never do such a thing but I wanted them to believe that I might as a way to avoid deportation, to embarrass them and cause a huge problem if I did so.

Half an hour later, I spotted him walking quickly, passing the cell and giving me a quick look without stopping. He seemed troubled, worried. The safety of the prisoners is the guards' responsibility, and if anything happened, they would be to blame. I knew that and depended on the fact that we had a common interest in clarifying this issue.

An hour later, three of them came, including the senior guard.

"Who told you that you are going to be sent back Monday?"

"A female officer, two days ago. She works upstairs, I guess."

"Maybe she misunderstood or maybe she was joking with you. Your flight is Monday, that is right, but to Canada, not to Syria."

"Joking! Is this something to joke about? I don't think she was. Maybe you are just telling me this to calm me down. I need to be sure please."

"We are telling you. Tomorrow is your flight to Canada."

Their faces showed how worried they were, and I had to resist the desire to smile. I dug into the anger I'd felt for the last two days.

"Great. I believe you. Can you please show me the ticket?"

The selfie guy said, "I will bring it to you, please don't do anything stupid." And I nodded my head, agreeing.

Five minutes later he was back, with some documents in his hand. He showed me through the bars, and I held onto the paper.

There was my name on top, and beneath were details of my flights, two of them: one China Airlines to Taipei, the other to Vancouver, Canada.

He kept trying to pull back the document but I wouldn't let go. I wanted to read those words over and over. Vancouver International Airport—Canada.

"That is enough," he said and pulled the paper back.

"Man," I said, "I wish today was tomorrow." I laughed, and so did he.

Tomorrow finally arrived, after 263 days—seven months at the airport and almost two months in jail, 6312 hours of waiting. Tomorrow had finally come, after seven years of fatigue, heat, hunger, fear, homelessness, illegality, hopelessness and sadness. Life fulfilled its promise: "I will make you happy," it had said, "safe and with a future, but first I will test you and make you stronger."

In the morning, I had a final cold-water shower; the night before I'd washed my clothes and had a shower too, but there was nothing wrong with one more. I hoped to make my hair look better—it had been nine months since I'd had a proper haircut—and I did not want to give a bad impression. How could I convince people that I wasn't a terrorist if I looked like one with my long hair and beard? The shower didn't help much, and I looked like someone on the run from the Middle Ages. I had one more trick: I used the shampoo my inmates had given me as a styling cream and there was some improvement. Nothing left but to stand next to the cell door and wait for them to call my name.

I kicked out all the negative and dark thoughts I had while waiting, the fear that they wouldn't call my name, that they would send me back, that something would go wrong—I should have checked my ticket one more time, just to make sure they'd spelled my name correctly.

Does my family know? I wondered. I can't wait to hear their voices. It was easy to imagine their happiness once they knew that I was on my way to Canada. At last, I'd finally done something to make them happy. I also couldn't wait to call my friends as well: Laurie, Stephen, Mr. Andrew and Dr. Osama. *Come on now! Are you kidding me? It's only two minutes since I last checked the time.*

But they finally came, all six of them in uniform, including some high-ranking officers. They called my name, asked me to sign a document confirming I'd received all my belongings. Then they handcuffed me.

"My glasses!" I shouted to the guards. It had been so long since I'd seen clearly, everything felt weird for a couple of minutes when I put them on for the first time.

Where are you now? I asked Other Hassan. I was looking at the empty seat next to me in the police van. I was hoping you would show yourself now. I understand you don't want to admit that I won and you lost. Other Hassan was not coming, and never would again. It's the Yin and Yang of Chinese philosophy, I thought. The main battle of our life is the one we win against ourselves, the weak and dark side of us that mocks and tempts us, pushing us to give up.

"Now I know how presidents feel," I told my escorts as we got out of the van. They took off the handcuffs, brought me a trolley and surrounded me: two in front, one on each side and two behind. Everyone was looking at us—me in a T-shirt, too-big jeans (I'd lost more weight), flip-flops and partially tamed long hair and beard— and the honour guard around me. Who is this guy? He looks messy and unimportant but he sure has a lot of bodyguards . . .

For this trip, I didn't have to wait in line, as they took me past a special counter and straight to the departure gate. There, they gave me back my cellphones. The one Laurie had sent me wasn't working. Damn it! I needed to make a call. Without much hope, I tried the Chinese one and it worked! "I love this phone," I said. "It never let me down, coming back from death every time I need it. It's the best phone China ever made."

Finally, I made the call I'd been waiting to make for years.

"Listen, don't cry," were the first words I said to my mother, "otherwise you will make me cry too, and I don't want to be weak in front of these guys." She cried anyway, as I knew she would. I did too, though I tried hard not to. My mother did not say much—"I love you. I miss you"—and passed the phone to Solaf and Ammar. I could feel their joy, a genuine happiness my family had missed for too long. For the first time in years, my call to my family was bringing them smiles, not tears, and that was priceless, even if there wasn't much time to talk. Then I texted each of my Avengers. I got on the plane without looking back or saying goodbye to the guards. From the plane, I saw all six of them lined up behind the glass, looking at me, and that was it.

I don't remember what the flight attendant looked like, but I do remember asking her for a cup of coffee and to keep it coming. I looked up to the left side of the sky through the small window, and he was there, my father. I've spoken to everyone but you, I said. I am safe now.

He smiled at me. I felt his words. It was hard and unique what you've done. Not the situation—all Syrians are going through the same—but the way you handled it. You remembered what I taught you, this is the difference in your story, not the story itself. One more thing—don't forget who you became during your march toward your dream, it is more important than the dream itself. Don't forget your family or your people. Don't forget those you left behind. There is no end, for as long as you are alive, the end is nothing but the start of a new beginning.

Part Three
.CA

Chapter Thirteen

O Canada

"IF YOU DIED, where you would like to be buried, Syria or Canada?" The question startled me; it had never crossed my mind before. This was a few months after I arrived in Canada, and I was sitting in Marion Botsford Fraser's car in Vancouver, watching the movement of pedestrians and traffic. She was interviewing me for a book she was writing about refugees. I stroked my beard and closed my eyes while I thought of my answer. The real question, hiding behind the one she'd asked, was about the concept of belonging and patriotism—what does home mean to you? To whom are you loyal? Which country do you love the most?

I considered my experiences and those of others. Refugees live with the conflict between their history and their future. Why can we not be proud of both, rather than to feel we are always betraying one or the other? We live with the accusations from the people we left behind that we have denied our homeland, sacrificed our obligations to them to save ourselves. I, and others like me, see the look of pity when I explain that I am a refugee, originally from Syria, and wonder how long we must live in our new country before those looks stop.

Syria is where I was born and raised, the land of my ancestors, my history, memories, family, friends and farm. I know our house there, the colour of its walls, the pictures that hang on the walls, the titles of the books in the library. Syria is the place of my father's grave, and I feel its pain with every shell that falls. I did not choose it, but it is part of my DNA.

Canada is where I find myself. It is my present and my future, the country where I can live, not only permanently, safely and legally, as was my dream at the airport; it is a land where I can live with rights, dignity, respect and with value as a human being. Canada is where I started getting used to saying "thank you" all the time, and "sorry" even if it's not my mistake. It's a country guided by rules and defined by kindness. I was not born or raised here, but I choose it to be part of my DNA too.

With all in that in my mind, I opened my eyes and said to Marion, "When I made a speech in Victoria, I introduced myself like this: 'My name is Hassan Al Kontar. I am a proud Syrian and I am a proud future Canadian.'

"When I die, I will make sure to be buried in both, half in Syria and half in Canada. I will also make sure not to be cremated. I don't want them to throw my ashes in the ocean—I would be worried that some would land on the beaches of Malaysia."

It was snowing in Whistler the day I arrived. After living in the desert for eleven years, then spending eight months at the mercy of air-conditioners, I suddenly realized how much I'd missed it. ("I'm from a mountain myself, I'm used to cold and the snow," became my usual answer to people who asked me what I thought about Whistler.) That first night, I couldn't sleep at all and kept running outside, alone in the dark singing Nina Simone's "Feeling Good." I couldn't stop dancing and grinning. *Be cool, man! You've seen it before, don't act like a kid.* But like the kid I'd been, I prayed for the snow to keep falling. When I was a child that was when the magic happened: school was cancelled, we got to watch TV, and our mother prepared the best special "snow day" food. White and clean, snow in Sweida meant happiness. My soul refused to listen to the exhaustion of my body, and I danced with my mother's voice singing in my head.

My Canadian godmother, my 007 and the leader of my Avenger team, Laurie hugged me at the airport and welcomed me into her home. I lived with her for six months, and became part of her family: her husband, George, and children Julia and Jaime took me into their warm, loving home. They, in turn, fell in love with the real Syrian meals I'd cook for them as a small thank you for all they'd done and were doing for me.

Like all Canadians, Laurie has the right to choose how to enjoy her life. While others travel, go to concerts and movies, take care of their home and family, Laurie chose a different path. She chose to make a difference, to show how one person can change someone's life. She gave and gives of her time and her children's time to take care of the children of others, offering love, peace and hope. She, Stephen and Mr. Andrew restored my faith in humanity and showed the power of individuals to make a difference and beat The System.

For fifty-nine days, the days I spent in the Malaysian jail, I said to myself each morning, If only I could have a cup of coffee, things would be so much easier. I don't like tea, especially when it is cold and served in a plastic bag that the guards would throw at you like a weapon if they didn't like you. Coffee brings back memories of my mother roasting and making it, of my father pouring it and welcoming guests on a cold day.

A few months after I arrived in Canada, I had an interview for a job at the Scandinave Spa bistro. The boss said, "We've heard that you like coffee. Tell us more about that."

"Let me put it this way," I answered, "my relationship with coffee

223

has been the longest and most serious relationship I have ever had, unfortunately. What you drink says a lot about your personality. For me, coffee is an important part of life and I think we should all enjoy it while we can. The day may come when you can no longer have it and then it will be all you can think about. Not because it's a need or because your life depends on it, but because it is a symbol of being a normal person, a suggestion of freedom."

"Done. The job is yours," he said.

You'd think that when you've achieved what you worked for—even if it is the basics of being legal and safe—you'd be focused on the future and what is next. For me, I returned to my memories, the bad and good ones, and was often haunted by the faces of those left behind. Sitting in my room in Whistler, with a beautiful snow-covered mountain view, surrounded by peace and quiet, I would hold my cup of coffee with both hands, tightly, as if someone was going to take it away or it might disappear, and remember the time when I didn't have the freedom to drink a cup of coffee any time I wanted. I remembered my cellmates in Abu Dhabi and Malaysia—I actually miss them— and wished I knew what happened to all of them.

While I don't ever want to return to the UAE, the place means something to me because what happened there is why I am where I am now. I'd like to go back, just once, to the place where I parked the car I lived in for years, to the streets I walked when homeless and hopeless. I want to look into the faces of the policemen and officers, holding my Canadian passport, to see if they would treat me differently now.

I'd like to go back to Malaysia, to meet my police case officer, the one who took off the handcuffs, gave me a cigarette and made coffee. "I looked hard into your case, and I found nothing. You are not a criminal, just having some bad luck," he'd said. I want to meet him one more time, in a café in Kuala Lumpur, and buy him a cup of coffee and return the favour—the favour of kindness in the middle of all this darkness.

When I stop thinking about the past and look to the future, it is my family I see. As an employee at the spa, I had free access to the beautiful outdoor hot baths and steam rooms, but it took me a month to try any of them. I wanted my family to be with me, and I couldn't enjoy it alone, knowing that they were living in misery while I was steaming. Whistler Village is like a souvenir snow globe, and I imagined my nephew and niece being there with me, dreamt of their reaction when they saw how beautiful it was. I didn't want to enjoy this beauty alone. I wanted to see my nephew, Medo, playing with a dog, a husky or a Golden Retriever, and I wanted to teach him how to ski.

Now that I live in Vancouver, I'd like to give Ammar and Tharaa's daughter, Jasmin, a kitten, and watch her grow up, not missing a lot of her childhood as I did with Medo. I want to meet my sister-in-law at long last.

Once I see them free, happy, and safe, I will start looking to have a future of my own, but not before that. It's a sacrifice I am ready to make any time, any day. What is the point of creating new lives if you haven't saved the lives of those you already have and care about? A man is not happy until his family is happy, a man is not free until his family is free, and a man is not safe until his family is safe.

In the Arab world, we believe that mothers live for one dream only, seeing their grandchildren, and we have a proverb: "The only thing more precious than my child is his child." My mother, Huda, has asked me the same questions since I've been in Canada: how is my health, am I eating well, and have I met anyone yet? When I say not yet, she starts mentioning what looks like a list of ladies I may be interested in. Now, after writing this book, my answer is one she may not like (and may get me in big trouble with her), "Huda, my love, I have a child now to carry my name. He's called *man@the_airport*."

Of course, I am grateful for the day jobs I've had since coming to Canada, but they are not what I want to do with my life. They pay the bills but don't feed the soul. After I arrived, I applied to every humanitarian organization and NGO in BC. I presented myself as a refugee advocate, my story and background, but with no success. It's been disheartening, but my time at the airport taught me perseverance, and I do what I can to leverage my social media experience and contacts to help those I can. Mostly, I want to tell the story of refugees. Laurie and I started Operation#NotForgotten, to help the refugees trapped on Manus and Nauru. I am trying to fulfill my promise to those people, the one I was unable to keep when the Australian TV program edited out my comments. MOSAIC, a BC NGO and one of Canada's largest settlement charities, now runs the project, which aims to provide safe resettlement through its Private Refugee Sponsorship Program.

Life is shaped by our priorities, and mine changed from employment to legal status to safety to sticking to my cause over the years in the UAE and Malaysia. When we achieve one priority and set another that is harder or better, it's easy to become greedy and angry when we don't get what we want. Worse, we may start blaming others for not having it. Whenever I go through some difficult times in Canada, about not finding the job I want, feeling down, lonely or homesick, I remind myself about my life's priority, and about the fight I had and the price I paid to get it, and it is enough to lift my mood. Do I need more? Do I need a better job? More money to be financially stable? Sure I do. Is it a priority? No, it is not. I will work for it, try and try again, but I am not going to forget what I already have.

Last year, I was invited to give a presentation at a workshop in Burnaby, BC, about the financial, social, emotional and financial employment challenges refugees face in their new countries. Before it started, there was a discussion and questions from some newcomers and refugees. Among them was a refugee from Afghanistan, who was having a difficult time hiding his anger. He didn't accept the fact that you need to start from scratch to build your career in a new country and that you need local experience to be accepted in some jobs. He also didn't accept that he was being asked to pay $500 to attend classes to get the certificate he needed.

I looked at him and understood how he felt, but I wanted to remind him of his priorities and how he should be more optimistic and thankful for not being in Kabul, and how many people in his country and around the world wished they could be where he was. "So what?" I said, "They want you to get the certificate. Pay the money, attend the class and get the damn certificate. Their roof, their rules. Play by them."

The celebrity and attention I received because of social media have been a mixed blessing. Yes, through it I found safety in a new home in a great country, but I also attracted hate, animosity and jealousy. I still receive abusive comments from Malaysians and people from Arab countries. With some celebrity comes trust issues; you're never sure if you are being approached because of who you are, or for what you can do for them. Sadly, like some of those people who tried to use me while I was at the airport, I have on occasion felt used in Canada by some groups who operate less for humanitarian reasons than for social prestige.

Recently a Syrian guy who was following me on Facebook launched a huge online personal attack, accusing me of using the refugee crisis for my own benefit and doing nothing for them. I normally don't block people—they have the right to speak—as I understand very well how frustrated they can be and what it means to feel helpless, so I give them a break with understanding. I take in what they say and don't respond. With this guy, I made an exception. Two days after his barrage of hate, he sent me a private message, asking me to use my connections to help get him into Canada. Attacking me in public, seeking help in private—this was definitely a trust issue. I blocked him.

The response from the Syrian community, both at home and abroad, has always been problematic. When I was at the airport, a well-known Facebook page for Syrians living in Canada posted something about me, only to delete it two hours later. The comments the post received were from Syrians who questioned my story, accusing me of many things and denying my right to come to Canada. Many Syrians, who find themselves safe and settled in Canada or other western countries, still play politics, supporting either the rebels or the current regime. Questioning the motives and veracity of new arrivals is commonplace.

On another occasion, an Arab radio station in the US called me for a phone interview. I accepted and during the broadcast, a Syrian man rang into the program. He was a refugee who'd been in the States with his wife and children for a few years. On air, he attacked me: "Why do all of you want to come to the USA or other western countries? Try an Arab country, they will take you in."

During the pandemic lockdown, a photo of Justin Trudeau with some Arabic text was trending and a friend sent it to me via WhatsApp. He couldn't believe what it said was true, and he wanted me to confirm it.

"Is it true that they are paying you to stay at home? Is it true that the transportation is free?"

"Yes, it's true," I typed.

"Man! What a country! What a lucky guy you are!"

"Yes, that is also true."

I was and am grateful to this country, and to the people who helped me to come here. Social media led me to them, and they saved my life. Social media led to global media attention, which fed social media support for my cause and the cause of Syrians everywhere. I have a huge debt, one that I am trying to repay by working for refugees and continuing to use social media to raise awareness of their plight. I may have disappointed some of those who supported me, and that saddens me. I am fortunate to have found peace. I refused to fight in the Syrian war, and now I won't fight other people's war, nor start a battle with people who have never done me any harm. In Canada, as in Malaysia, I still have the right to say no.

In one of his check-up calls to me at KLIA2, Jehad said, "Man, even if you were made of iron, you would have been melted down by now!" I laughed but didn't answer. I knew the answer but I kept it to myself. If I had spoken what was in my heart, I would have said, "During my whole life, I was waiting for something. I knew it was coming, but I did not know what it would be. Now I do. It's this: with every problem I had, I was searching for the logic behind it, and for a long time none of it made sense. Now those years of problems do. All that I've been through is lining up to make perfect sense. Place and time don't matter anymore. Achieving my goal is what matters, not whether I am clean or dirty, hungry, thirsty, tired or not; it doesn't matter if I am sleeping on a king-sized bed or on a chair or on the floor. For years, I lost myself and now I've found me again. I am once again a man with a purpose, and what happened to me is giving my life meaning—to tell the story and show the world who the real Syrians are. Jehad, who we become during our journey towards our dreams is more important than the dream itself. It doesn't matter anymore what is going to happen to me on a personal level. I've succeeded already by telling the story. I stood up and said no. I'm in love with and proud of what I am doing. I believe in what I am doing. Death may come sooner or later—it makes absolutely no difference. I am no longer Hassan only, I am now the man at the airport. Iron will melt down at a certain temperature, but there is no breaking point for a human soul with a cause to fight for. Iron will give up and melt once it reaches its limit, but there is no giving up if you have faith in what are you doing. Life offers only one option— to wake up every morning, smile no matter what, and start chasing your dream all over again."

Now I know what the olive trees in our farm were trying to teach me, and why my father took me with him to tend them. You plant the trees, you water them and care for them, and for years they give you nothing. Weeks of work, for years, and no olives, no income. But the farmers understand that—it's a pledge between them and the trees. It's how life works, not asking for instant results and proof that what you are doing is right. Stay patient, keep watering and caring—the trees will start giving. The olives. The peace.

Postscript

AS THIS BOOK is going to print, I have accepted a job offer from the Canadian Red Cross to work as an Emergency Care Worker. And, after years of neglect, my family has managed to harvest olives at our farm for the first time since 2011. It was a good season—eleven tanks in total, each weighing sixteen kilograms. After Ammar called to tell me the news, I was proud of him for keeping our father's legacy.